Railway Bylines

Annual
Number 2

Pastoral Northumberland... J21 0-6-0 No.65033 is being turned at Reedsmouth, on the delightful Border Counties line. The date is August 1961. PHOTOGRAPH: I.JOHNSON

Edited By
Martin Smith

Editor
Martin Smith

Cover. Beattie Well tank with a rake of clay wagons on route to Wadebridge. PHOTOGRAPH: B.P. HOPER COLLECTION
Right. J67 0-6-0T No.68492 at St.Margaret's shed in Edinburgh on 10 May 1952. The engine was used on the Lauder branch which had a punitive axle-weight limit and so, to minimise the J67's axle-weight, it ran with empty tanks and carried its water in a tender. The activities of the J67s and J69s in Scotland was the subject of an article in the October 1998 issue of *Railway Bylines* magazine. PHOTOGRAPH: J.ROBERTSON; B. P. HOPER COLLECTION
Below. Burnham on Sea - 12 August 1953. PHOTOGRAPH: IVO PETERS

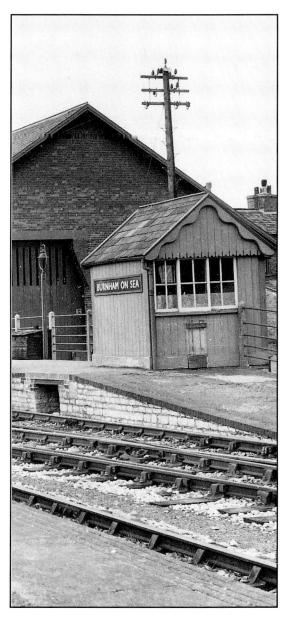

Railway Bylines

Welcome to the second RAILWAY BYLINES ANNUAL, our latest king-size dip into what might be termed the 'Minor Railways Selection Box'. Regular readers of RAILWAY BYLINES magazine - our monthly journal - will know the sort of things to expect during the course of the next ninety-odd pages: rural branch lines, industrial systems, narrow gauge, and other unjustly overlooked aspects of Britain's railway network.

One advantage of the 'Annual' format is that we can include articles which are a little too lengthy for an ordinary edition of the magazine. Such is the case with the **Tees Valley Railway** - the formal title of the branch line from Barnard Castle to Middleton-in-Teesdale - which is one of the principal subjects in this tome. As our researches unearthed all sorts of goodies, and as the branch has never been the subject of a detailed article in the railway press (at least, to the best of our knowledge), we felt that a longer feature was justifiable as it would enable us to present much that is 'new' to most readers. Or so we hope!

We have also expended much ink on a sort of double whammy, which deals with, not one, but two collieries in Yorkshire - **Emley Moor and Park Mill Collieries.** These two pits were within a mile and a half of each other, near the BR branch line to Clayton West, and the full story is brought to you by one of our regular contributors, Adrian Booth. Young Mr.Booth told us that he made several special trips to the two collieries at all times of year, in all winds and weathers, to study and record the scene. But we weren't altogether convinced by his tales of devotion to duty, as Emley Moor and Park Mill collieries aren't a million miles from Huddersfield, and Mr.B just happens to be a keen Huddersfield Town supporter. Suspicious souls that we are, we looked through old Huddersfield Town fixture lists and, as we half expected, every one of Mr.B's visits to Emley Moor and Park Mill collieries on a Saturday morning just happened to coincide with Huddersfield having a home game in the afternoon. You've been rumbled, young man...

The other 'well filled' portion of our selection box deals with **LMS Sentinels.** In his article, Bill Aves deals in his usual thorough manner with the LMS's Sentinel shunting locomotives *and* steam railcars. Once again, we smugly consider that this feature treads fairly new ground, as not much has previously been said in the railway press about these machines, especially the activities of the railcars.

Elsewhere in these pages, we try to provide something for everybody. We have BR and non-BR, standard gauge and narrow gauge, ancient and modern, the pretty and the functional, locomotives and infrastructure. All in all, its a sort of railway version of 'The Good, The Bad and The Ugly'. We hope you like what's on offer. If you enjoy our rummage through the bits that other railway magazines don't reach, remember that there is a 56-page helping of this sort of fare every single month in RAILWAY BYLINES magazine.

Railway Bylines

**Published by
Irwell Press**
59A, High Street,
Clophill, Bedfordshire
MK45 4BE
Tel:- 0181 363 5285
Fax:- 0181 373 9872
**Printed & Bound
in the United Kingdom
by The Amadeus press
Huddersfield
Yorkshire, 1998**

Middleton-in-Teesdale station, the terminus of the branch from Barnard Castle, was an absolute delight, perched on the hillside above the south-west bank of the River Tees. In this picture the river can just be discerned in the valley below the station. The station was in Yorkshire, but the town (which was half a mile or so distant) was in County Durham - the eastern outskirts of the town can be seen in the mid-distance. On 25 October 1952, G5 0-4-4T No.67273 of West Auckland shed stands in the station with a two-coach train; this was a typical branch ensemble of the period. The large building at the left-hand end of the platform is the station master's house. In the foreground can be seen the alignment of the siding which formerly served Ord & Maddison's quarries farther up Teesdale; the siding had been lifted earlier in 1952. PHOTOGRAPH: J.W.ARMSTRONG TRUST

Today, the valley of the River Tees northward from the town of Barnard Castle - in what is now the south-west corner of County Durham is a well-known beauty spot which attracts many visitors, with the tourist industry making a very useful contribution to the local economy. However, in the mid-1800s the word 'tourism' was all but unheard of, and the majority of the people living in Teesdale were accustomed to ekeing out an erratic and precarious existence by whatever means the land offered. It mattered little to most of the locals that Sir Walter Scott's *Rokeby* had been drawn from their part of

THE TEES VALLEY RAILWAY
The Barnard Castle to Middleton in Teesdale branch

by Oswald J.Barker and Bryan L.Wilson

'Middleton is a thriving and beautifully situated little town, and the busy centre of a district teeming with mineral riches, which require but the magic wand of industrial enterprise to touch them, to become sources of wealth, untold happiness and prosperity' (Darlington and Stockton Times, Saturday 15 October 1864)

Teesdale, as although the literary connection might have generated local pride in some quarters, it did not help with the serious matter of putting food on the table. Consequently, when it was suggested in the early 1860s that Teesdale might be exploited for its mineral riches, thereby creating opportunities for employment, the idea was greeted with considerable local enthusiasm. The exploitation of the area's mineral

The nominal starting point for Middleton-in-Teesdale branch trains was Barnard Castle, though since pre-war times most of the branch trains ran through to and from Darlington or Durham. Consequently, the bay platform at the western end of Barnard Castle station was normally used, not for arrivals and departures, but for 'holding' a branch train, or for longer than usual layovers, while the main through platform was occupied. On 23 July 1957, G5 0-4-4T No.67320 of Durham shed is held in the bay with the 11.02am to Middleton-in-Teesdale. Standard Class 4 2-6-0 No.76020 hauls a westbound freight through the station - it is heading towards Kirkby Stephen via the Stainmore Line. All that is seen here has gone - the site of Barnard Castle station is now part of a Glaxo factory. PHOTOGRAPH: IAN S.CARR

The east end of Barnard Castle *circa* 1949/50. One can clearly see the somewhat unusual arrangement of one through platform to cope with trains in both directions - the through platform is the one which is partially covered by the overall roof. The platform road on the left is a dead-end bay, used principally by trains to and from Bishop Auckland. A G5 0-4-4T and a train of vintage stock wait in the bay, while an 0-6-0 (possibly a J21) waits with an eastbound train at the through platform. In the distance one can see the signal box near the west end of the station. PHOTOGRAPH: W.A.CAMWELL

wealth required improved means of transportation which, inevitably for the period, meant a railway. As was intended, the railway which was duly built along Teesdale became closely allied to the quarrying industry, but in addition to tapping the 'mineral riches', it was also to play a vital role on more than one occasion in the construction of reservoirs in Baldersdale and Lunedale. Furthermore, the railway brought tourists to and from Teesdale - often the same day - and it also developed a steady, if not spectacular, income from its regular passenger traffic. The Teesdale railway was the final development of the railway system in the area; so let us now look to the hills.

The local railway map

The principal town in the immediate area was Barnard Castle. It became rail connected on 8 July 1856 when the Darlington & Barnard Castle Railway opened its line from a junction with the Stockton & Darlington Railway at Hopetown, just to the west of Darlington. To quote William Weaver Tomlinson, '...there was no little rejoicing at Barnard Castle on that day',

The construction of the railway to Barnard Castle was no mean achievement, but the prospect of continuing the line westwards from the town, across inhospitable Pennine country, was an altogether different matter. Nevertheless, the South Durham & Lancashire Union Railway had such an aim in mind - the company considered that worthwhile revenue could be forthcoming from the transportation of iron ore from Ulverston, in north-west Lancashire, to the furnaces at Middlesbrough and taking coal and coke in the opposite direction. The SD&LUR's proposed railway across the Pennines - running by way of Kirkby Stephen to Tebay - received its

Act of Parliament on 13 July 1857. Given the nature of the terrain it had to cross, construction was very difficult, yet the line was completed within less than four years - it opened as far as Barras for mineral traffic on 26 March 1861 and to Kirkby Stephen (again, only for minerals) on 4 July. Passenger services commenced on 8 August.

At Barnard Castle, the terminus of the Darlington & Barnard Castle Railway was superseded by a new through station on the SD&LUR line. The old terminus was subsequently given over to goods traffic - a common fate, in those days, for redundant passenger stations. The SD&LUR became popularly known as the 'Stainmore Line', after its famous summit at Stainmore which, at 1,370ft above sea level, was the second highest on a standard gauge line in England and the third highest in Britain.

Into Teesdale

At a public meeting at the Rose and Crown in Middleton-in-Teesdale on 8 October 1864, it was formally proposed to promote a railway from '...the Stockton & Darlington line east of Lartington, and passing along the south bank of the Tees to Middleton...'. The line was promoted as the Tees Valley Railway. The meeting was reported in the *Darlington and Stockton Times* on 15 October 1864, the newspaper explaining that: *'Middleton is a thriving and beautifully situated little town, and the busy centre of a district teeming with mineral riches, which require but the magic wand of industrial enterprise to touch them, to become sources of wealth, untold happiness and prosperity... there can be no doubt that when the contemplated line is opened a great impetus will be given to certain branches of industrial occupation, and the opening up of channels of remunerative employment to hundreds of our labouring population'.*

The prospectus for the Tees Valley Railway noted that the provisional directors were:
Rev.Thomas Witham of Lartington Hall (Chairman)
Henry Pease M.P. of Pierremont, Darlington
W.T.Scarth of Kelverston Hall

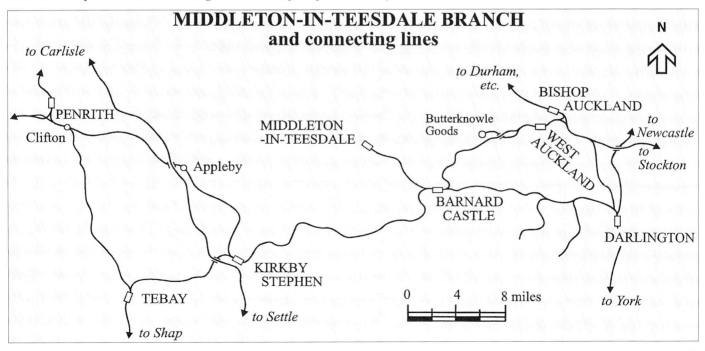

MIDDLETON-IN-TEESDALE BRANCH and connecting lines

N

to Carlisle

PENRITH

Clifton

Appleby

to Durham, etc.

BISHOP AUCKLAND

to Newcastle

to Stockton

MIDDLETON -IN-TEESDALE

Butterknowle Goods

WEST AUCKLAND

BARNARD CASTLE

DARLINGTON

TEBAY

KIRKBY STEPHEN

to Settle

to Shap

0   4   8 miles

to York

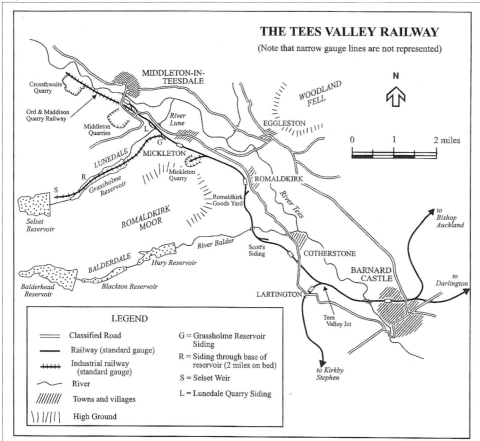

THE TEES VALLEY RAILWAY
(Note that narrow gauge lines are not represented)

LEGEND

Classified Road	G = Grassholme Reservoir Siding
Railway (standard gauge)	R = Siding through base of reservoir (2 miles on bed)
Industrial railway (standard gauge)	S = Selset Weir
River	L = Lunedale Quarry Siding
Towns and villages	
High Ground	

Isaac Wilson of Nunthorpe Hall
John Whitwell, Mayor of Kendal
Thomas MacNay of Darlington
Thompson Richardson of Barnard Castle
Robert Thompson of Darlington
W.R.Innes Hopkins of Elton Hall
J.Monro of Barnard Castle
Henry Fell Pease of Brinkburn, Darlington
James Hopkins of Middlesbrough
George Brown of Barnard Castle
Thomas Vaughan of Middlesbrough
Jacob Allison of Cotherstone
H.K.Spark of Greenbank, Darlington
The company secretary was Lancelot Railton of Barnard Castle

It will be noted that two members of the Pease family were among the provisional directors. The Peases were highly influential local industrialists with the proverbial irons in several fires; the family had had an involvement with railways since the formative days of the Stockton & Darlington, and Henry Pease, along with his father, Edward, and two brothers, Edward Jnr. and Joseph, had been present at the trial run of the Stockton & Darlington Railway's famous LOCOMOTION at Shildon in September 1825. Henry Pease was also a director of various other railway companies in the north-east, among them the Middlesbrough & Redcar Railway, the Wear Valley Railway and, later, the North Eastern Railway. (Four other members of the family were also directors of the NER at various times, and one - Sir Joseph Whitwill Pease - served as Chairman from 1895 to 1902).

The Tees Valley Railway prospectus noted that the company's capital was £50,000 in 2,000 shares of £25 each. In typical fashion, it waxed lyrical about the prospects for the company: *'The length of the proposed Tees Valley Railway will be about seven miles. It commences at a Junction with the South Durham and Lanca-*

shire Union Railway a little to the west of the Tees Viaduct, near Barnard Castle, and passing along the valley of the Tees, via Lartington, Cotherstone, Romaldkirk, Eggleston and Mickleton, terminates at Middleton-in-Teesdale.

The want of Railway communication with the higher parts of Teesdale has long been felt, by the inhabitants of the district and the public generally, and numerous attempts have been made to attain this desideratum, all of which have hitherto proved unsuccessful from the expensive character of the Lines projected.

The Tees Valley has been carefully surveyed and levelled by Messrs. Nimmo and MacNay, C.E., Westminster, who have succeeded in laying out a Railway, the works of which are of remarkably easy character, the Line running almost along the surface by easy gradients for the whole distance. Estimates have been made on a liberal scale, based upon the actual cost of similar works in the neighbourhood, which show that the whole works may be completed, and the Line ready for use, for a sum not exceeding £50,000.

A report on the mineral resources of Teesdale was made some years ago by T.E.Forster Esq, Mining Engineer, from which it appears that ironstone of a rich quality is found on the extensive estates of the Duke of Cleveland in this locality. Middleton-in-Teesdale is the centre of a large lead mining and lead smelting district. The proposed Railway will, by means of the Stockton & Darlington Line, open this district to the East and West Coasts, and to the principal towns in England. To the numerous tourists who frequent this valley it will afford access to the charming and romantic scenery at Cotherstone, Baldersdale, Middleton, High Force and Cauldron Snout. In addition to Passengers and Merchandise, the traffic of the Line will consist of Coal,

Coke, Lime and other Minerals, together with Agricultural Produce, and at the moderate computation of £17 per mile per week a dividend of upwards of 6 per cent per annum would be realised. For purposes of comparison, the average weekly receipts on the following Railways are:
Stockton & Darlington - £65 per mile
Maryport & Carlisle - £56 per mile
Furness Railway - £64 per mile
Whitehaven Junction - £81 per mile
Blyth & Tyne - £38 per mile
Whitehaven & Furness - £29 per mile
Deeside Railway - £36 per mile

The landowners and inhabitants of the Valley are favourable to the project... and with a view to economy in working, powers will be taken in the Act for the Stockton & Darlington Railway Company to work the Line'.

The promoters made no secret of the fact that the railway was envisaged as part of a greater scheme. It was anticipated that the line would ultimately extend to Alston - a hugely ambitious idea, given the extremely challenging nature of the terrain between Middleton-in-Teesdale and Alston - where it would link up with the line to Haltwhistle; this would, in theory, have provided a route by which the mineral produce of Teesdale could have been taken to the industrial centres of Cumberland. But the Alston extension was not to be.

The Tees Valley Railway received the Royal Assent on 19 June 1865 and the first sod was ceremonially cut at Middleton-in-Teesdale by the Duke of Cleveland, one of the principal local landowners, on 9 November 1865. The construction of the railway was undertaken by a contractor named Boulton who had tendered £28,244.11s.6d, part of which was to be paid in the form of shares (a fairly common arrangement of the period); when the railway company had discussed the various tenders earlier in 1865, a slightly less expensive offer from a contractor named Appleby (£27,537) had been on the table, but it had been considered that Mr.Appleby might not have been able to complete the job satisfactorily.

The Tees Valley Railway invited the North Eastern Railway to subscribe to the undertaking, and the matter was discussed by the latter's directors on 26 April 1863: *'...upon consideration, and looking at the fact that the Stockton & Darlington Company having for many years contemplated securing the control of any line that might be formed into the Tees Valley, this Committee is of the opinion that the present is a favourable opportunity of accomplishing that object and encouraging local effort, and recommends that a contribution be made under proper regulations for guarding the interests of this Company, or the Committee will be prepared to authorize an appeal to the Darlington Shareholders to contribute individually under suitable arrangements as to the working of the line'.*

The NER duly proposed a subscription of £25,000, providing that it could nominate five of the directors on the Tees Valley board. This was a commonplace procedure but, somewhat mysteriously, the five directors nominated by the NER - Messrs. Henry Pease, Henry Fell Pease, John

Dixon, Thomas MacNay and Robert Thompson - had previously been appointed by the Tees Valley itself.

During the construction of the railway, the Tees Valley company necessarily attended to the various matters which cropped up. The company records reveal much about the everyday goings on - the very minutiae - of a small, independent railway company; for example, at a meeting on 3 February 1866 the directors agreed: '...that a station shall be provided at Cotherston (sic) for passengers; and that a station be provided at Romaldkirk for passengers, coal and lime; and a station at Mickleton for passengers, goods, lime and coals...'. The directors' minutes dated 3 March 1866 record that: '...Engineers are requested to report upon a means of obtaining water to the fields through which the railway will pass behind Cotherston...the Engineer reported that no passing places are required at present...'. On 7 April 1866: '...Engineer is requested to ascertain the views and wishes of the inhabitants of Cotherston as to the heights and widths of the bridges...'. And on 7 July 1866: '...Estimate of proposed road to the station at Romaldkirk: length of new road - 150 yards; metalling - 300 cu.yds. @ 5/- - £75.0.0; fencing - 209 linear yards - £20.18.0; curb on footpath - 202 feet @ 1/- - £10.2.0; gravel - £5.12.6; land - £56.0.0; Total - £167.12.6'.

At some stage, thoughts were given to purchasing the necessary land and constructing the bridges etc to allow for a second line of rails to be laid at a future date (this, too, was fairly commonplace, many minor railways all over Britain being built with the possibility of future doubling in mind). In the case of the Tees Valley Railway, the figures were:
Extra land 11¼ acres @ £160: £1,800
4 public road overbridges: £520

8 occupation overbridges: £1,000
Viaducts: £5,090
Contingencies @ 10% of total:- £509
Grand total - £5,599
As things turned out, the option of constructing for a double-track line was not taken up.

Almost inevitably, the railway company did not always see eye to eye with all the locals. One source of dispute concerned seven road bridges in the parish of Romaldkirk which were being prepared for construction - it was alleged that the proposed works for these bridges were not in accordance with what had been sanctioned, as in most cases their abutments would protrude into the roadway far more than had been approved; in one case a road would be reduced from 25ft to 20ft in width, and in another from 20ft to 14ft. The Board of Trade was asked to adjudicate, and in his report dated 13 July 1866, Captain Rich refused to sanction the railway company's departure from the dimensions which had been laid down by the Act of Parliament. Captain Rich did not seem particularly impressed with the manner in which the railway company had conducted its business, remarking rather pointedly that: 'The surveyors in charge of these roads appear to be the common farmers of the neighbourhood and in some cases labourers, who were employed breaking the stones for making the roads, and certainly not proper judges to sanction the proposed alterations'.

Returning to more routine corporate matters, at a meeting of the Tees Valley Railway's directors on 1 December 1866 it was noted that: '...goods shed at Middleton is approved...the passenger platform is to accommodate five carriages...50 feet diameter turntable approved...engine shed is of a length sufficient for one engine and tender...'.

At the same meeting it was noted that: '...Mr.Appleby's tender for the construction of the stations at Cotherston and Mickleton be accepted, amounting to £190.0.0 each...'. Also that: '...the contractors have applied to have the junction with the South Durham line laid in as early as possible as they wish to get ballast along the line...'. On 15 December 1866: '...no coal drops be provided at present at Cotherstone and that depots with two holes (coal drops) be provided at Mickleton...'. On 9 February 1867 it was: '...resolved that the tender of Mr.Hepworth be accepted for works at Middleton-in-Teesdale: construction of the goods shed - £297.16.0; the depots - £183.2.0; the weighhouse - £59.12.0; passenger station and house if built of stone - £666.0.0; passenger station and house if built of brick - £717.13.0...'. The turntable at Middleton was also discussed, the directors noting that: '...the engineers are requested to ask for a tender from the Darlington Forge Company for a 45 feet turntable as well as for a 50 feet one....'. Staffing was discussed on 22 February 1868: '...it is agreed that Henry Wane be appointed to the Level Crossing at Romaldkirk and that Marmaduke Allan be appointed Porter at Middleton for the goods and general business...regarding the proposed appointment of John Nelson to Mickleton, it happens that the person already appointed will do all that is necessary at that place...'.

The TVR directors sent an inspection party to the unfinished line on 28 March 1868; it was duly reported that: '...as to the siding asked for at Cotherstone, we decline to give any promise for this accommodation at present...the iron handrailing to be put on the Balder Viaduct is not begun with, but the Engineer says it is ready and they will cause it to be proceeded with immediately... The cottage at Romaldkirk is in a very un-

After arrived at Barnard Castle with the 11.40am Middleton-in-Teesdale to Bishop Auckland train on 24 July 1957, G5 No.67258 was detached so that it could take on water. It is seen at the east end of Barnard Castle station, running back to join its train.
PHOTOGRAPH: IAN S.CARR

finished state, and we directed that a proper legal notice be served upon Mr.Appleby the contractor at once...Mickleton station is also in an unfinished state...we have authorised the Secretary to order three clocks for the Stations which it appears can be obtained at £5.15.0 each...'.

Inspection and opening

As with all passenger carrying public railways in Britain, the Tees Valley Railway had to be approved by the Board of Trade before it could legally convey any fare-paying passengers. The obligatory inspection for the BoT was conducted by Lt-Col.Hutchinson, who reported on 1 May 1868. His report kicked off with the customary description of the works:

'The line is single throughout with sidings at Mickleton and Middleton... the rails are double-headed and weigh 55lbs per yard... the chairs weigh only 23½lbs each and are secured to the sleepers by two iron spikes and one oak trenail...the sleepers are of creosoted Memel timber... (The lightness

394.—TEES VALLEY.

Incorporated by 28 Vic., cap. 91 (19th June, 1865), to construct a line from the South Durham, at Lartington, to Middleton-in-Teesdale. Length, 7 miles. Capital, 50,000*l.* in 25*l.* shares, and 16,000*l.* on loan. Working arrangements with North Eastern, which subscribes 25,000*l.* Opened.

No. of Directors—9 ; quorum, 3. *Qualification,* 500*l.*

DIRECTORS:

Chairman—The Rev. THOMAS WITHAM, Lartington Hall.

Henry Pease, Esq., Pierremont, Darlington. | Robert Thompson, Esq., Darlington.
W. T. Scarth, Esq., Keverston Hall. | Henry Fell Pease, Esq., Brinkburn, Darlington.
Thomas MacNay, Esq., Darlington. |
Thompson Richardson, Esq., Barnard Castle. |

OFFICERS.—Sec., Lancelot Railton, Barnard Castle ; Treasurers, J. and J. W. Pease, Darlington ; Engs.. Nimmo and MacNay, C.E., 21, Abingdon Street, Westminster, S.W. ; Solicitor, R. T. Richardson, Barnard Castle ; London Bankers, Dimsdale, Fowler, and Barnard, 50, Cornhill, E,C.

Offices—Witham Testimonial Buildings, Barnard Castle.

The who's who of the Tees Valley Railway Company, as given in the 1869 edition of *Bradshaw's Shareholders' Guide*

of the chairs was emphasised in Hutchinson's report, but it was noted that as '...a portion of the permanent way was laid before the requirements of the Board of Trade were announced and also as the traffic on the branch is not likely to be of a heavy character...', the chairs would be acceptable as a short-term measure). *There are engine turntables at Barnard Castle and Middleton... There are three stations, viz. Cotherstone, Mickleton and Middleton and one public road authorized level crossing provided with lodge, gates and signals. The fencing is post and rail. The steepest gradient has an inclination of 1 in 77 and the sharpest curve a radius of 27 chains; the deepest cutting is 28 feet deep and the highest embankment 36 feet high.*

There are 7 overbridges, all of stone and brick with the exception of one built entirely of timber. The underbridges are 21 in number. There are also two viaducts over the Balder and Lune Rivers - the former has 9 arches, the span being 30ft, the latter 5 arches with a span of 50ft'.

Lt-Col.Hutchinson noted certain deficiencies: *'Tees Valley Junction - the arrival signals for Tees Valley and Bowes passenger lines should interlock with the station signal and carriage shed signal; a clock is wanted in the signalbox. Iron bridges - many short bolts require removal and replacing by longer ones. Mickleton Station - points to be weighted so as to be right for the main line. Authorised level crossing - distant signal towards Middleton is visible from only 215 yards to an approaching driver though the gradient is falling sharply towards the crossing; the signal must be removed to a more conspicuous position. Middleton Station - chock blocks on sidings have been placed too near the passenger line; spring buffer stops are required at the end of platform; a ramp must be substituted for steps at the east end of the platform; the distant and goods signals must be interlocked; the clock is not visible from the platform'.* Because of these deficiencies, Hutchinson declined to recommend that the line be opened to passenger traffic.

On same day as conducting his inspection of the Tees Valley line, Lt-Col.Hutchinson investigated a complaint from local residents that: '...at a bridge close to the viaduct over the Lune, there is a danger arising from horses taking fright at approaching trains'. There was also a complaint: '...as to the scour on the piers of this bridge created by the position of the piers of the viaduct'. However, Hutchinson noted that the relevant parties had reached 'a mutually satisfactory' arrangement, though he did not explain what this involved.

As for the deficiencies which prevented the railway from being opened, the Tees

Middleton-in-Teesdale branch trains leaving Barnard Castle used the Stainmore Line for the first mile or so before the actual branch diverged. The section between Barnard Castle and the junction incorporated two viaducts; one of these crossed the River Tees - it was 244 yards in length and had a maximum height of 132ft. In common with the other viaducts on the Stainmore Line, the Tees Viaduct was designed by Thomas Bouch; it proved to be rather more durable than certain other Bouch structures, particularly the first Tay Bridge. The ironwork for the lattice girders of the Tees Viaduct was supplied by Kennaird & Co, and the masonry work for the stone piers was undertaken by D.P.Appleby; the final bill for the construction of the viaduct was £25,119. PHOTOGRAPH: J.W.ARMSTRONG

The Middleton-in-Teesdale branch parted company with the Stainmore Line at Tees Valley Junction, a mile or so west of Barnard Castle station. Here, we are looking west towards the junction and its signal box. Beyond the junction, the branch ran parallel to the Stainmore Line for about a mile before heading northwards to Middleton. PHOTOGRAPH: J.W.ARMSTRONG TRUST

Valley company rectified matters with commendable haste and the line was ready for opening within a week and a half. The grand ceremonial opening took place on Tuesday 12 May 1868, the directors and railway officials leaving Darlington by train at 1.00pm train to be joined at Barnard Castle by a local party. The train proceeded to Middleton-in-Teesdale, where the dignitaries disembarked and walked in procession, preceded by two bands, to the London Lead Company's school room, where a tea was provided by the Working Men's Reading Room Society. The directors returned to Barnard Castle at 3.30pm to attend a ceremonial banquet at the Kings Head Hotel.

The public opening of the railway took place the following day, Wednesday 13 May 1868.

The route

A journey along the Tees Valley branch nominally started at Barnard Castle station. Although this station was on a double-track through line, it had only one through platform face; that said, there was a dead-end bay behind each end of the through platform, but as the years progressed the bay at the west end was of diminishing usefulness for Tees Valley trains as fewer and fewer of them started or terminated at Barnard Castle - by the 1930s most ran through to or from Darlington, Bishop Auckland or Durham, and the bay at Barnard Castle was used principally for 'holding' a train while another occupied the main platform.

We referred to the line through Barnard Castle station being double track. However, this was not originally the case, as when the Stainmore line was opened in 1861 it had only a single track - doubling of the section between Barnard Castle and Tees Valley Junction was authorised on 2 May 1866 and the work was completed later that year, some two years or so before it had to deal with additional traffic on the Tees Valley branch.

For the first mile or so westwards from Barnard Castle, the Tees Valley branch trains used the Stainmore line. The first important feature on this section of line was Percy Beck viaduct, 260ft long, 66ft high, with eight spans, immediately to the west of Barnard Castle station. Three-quarters of a mile to the west the railway crossed the slender Tees Viaduct, which was 732ft long, 132ft high, and had four stone piers supporting the lattice girder superstructure. The railway embarked on a climb of 1 in 70 towards Tees Valley Junction - this was the point, 1 mile 5 chains west of Barnard Castle, where the single-track Tees Valley branch diverged from the Stainmore line. It was later agreed that the cost of signalling at the junction (a total of £493.19.10) be split between the NER, who paid two-thirds, and the Tees Valley Railway, who paid one-third.

Like the other intermediate stations on the Middleton-in-Teesdale branch, Cotherstone was little altered during its 96-year life. That said, although it used to be kept in a very smart condition, after its relegation in status to that of an unstaffed halt (in 1954) there was nobody to look after it and, inevitably, it became rather tatty. This picture is taken in 'unstaffed' days. PHOTOGRAPH: J.W.ARMSTRONG TRUST

A8 4-6-2T No.69863 approaches Romaldkirk with the 5.53pm from Middleton-in-Teesdale to Sunderland on 27 July 1957. The open landscape in the distance - looking across to Monks Moor, Middleton Common and Eggleston Common - is typical of upper Teesdale. PHOTOGRAPH: IAN S.CARR

For about a mile west of the junction, the Tees Valley branch and the Stainmore line ran parallel with each other, the branch being on the north side on the alignment of a former mineral line. The original intention had been that the branch should join the Stainmore line a mile or so farther west, but the resiting of the junction nearer Barnard Castle avoided the necessity of a staff section at the originally intended junction.

As the Stainmore line curved to the south, still climbing, near Lartington Hall,

the branch headed north-westwards on its own course. Lartington Hall, incidentally, was once the residence of Rev.Thomas Witham, who had done much to promote the Tees Valley Railway and was its first chairman; he was also a director of the Darlington & Barnard Castle and the South Durham & Lancashire Union Railways. In a report of the opening of the railway in May 1868, the *Teesdale Mercury* opined that Rev.Witham's '...munificence is exhibited in the improvements he has effected for the benefit of cottagers on the

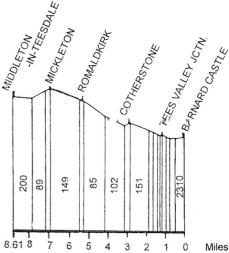

estate, and his good taste is apparent in the exquisite embellishments of the interior and exterior of his mansion'.

The first station along the branch was **Cotherstone** (2m 68ch from Barnard Castle); it was on the north side of the bridge carrying the railway over the Barnard Castle-Middleton road (now the B6277), and was almost ½-mile from the actual village. Somewhat mysteriously, in 1906 the spelling of the station name in the public timetables was changed to 'Cotherston', but the letter 'e' was reinstated in 1914. The station had a single platform and was devoid of a passing loop - there were, in fact, no passing places anywhere along the branch; the single-storey platform building offered somewhat modest facilities. There was one goods siding, alongside which were cattle pens - the provision of facilities for dealing with cattle was to be expected, as the locality was renowned for its dairy products, particularly Cotherstone Cheese, which was said to rival Stilton in flavour.

Romaldkirk station in North Eastern Railway days, looking north across the level crossing. The station did *not* open with the line - it was added a month or so later. Romaldkirk was a block post with signals, but did not have a crossing loop (there were no crossing loops anywhere on the branch); the block post was intended simply to break up the eight-mile section between Tees Valley Junction and Middleton, thereby enabling trains to follow one another more closely, though in practice that facility was not required very often. We see single crossing gates for the country road and oil lamps on the platform.

The Middleton-in-Teesdale branch was often used as a running-in turn for locomotives fresh from Darlington Works. In April 1957, Standard Class 2 2-6-2T No.84024 was brand new ex-works, and was being run in before its dispatch to the Southern Region. It is propelling a train away from Romaldkirk, heading for Barnard Castle and Darlington. PHOTOGRAPH: J.W.ARMSTRONG TRUST

In 1884, a siding 'for 14 trucks and an engine' was installed a little over ¾-mile to the north-west of Cotherstone for the benefit of the contractors, Messrs.W.Scott, who were engaged on the construction of Hury Reservoir for the Middlesbrough Water Works. A new ground frame with six levers was provided to control movements to and from the siding. The contractor's

siding - invariably referred to as Scott's Siding - fell into disuse when Hury Reservoir was completed, but was brought into use again in 1893 in connection with the construction of Blackton Reservoir, at the western end of Hury Reservoir. After the completion of Blackton Reservoir in autumn 1896, the siding was removed. (Another major reservoir - Balderhead Reser-

voir - was constructed nearby in 1961-65, but this had no railway involvement).

The railway continued northwards, climbing at 1 in 102 then 1 in 85, and crossed the River Balder on a splendid viaduct which had nine arches, each of 30ft span, and a maximum height of 100ft. The viaduct is stated to have cost 'a little under £5,000' to construct. By the mid-1870s

Middleton-in-Teesdale branch signal boxes and ground frames

N.B: In some cases, the precise date on which a signal box or ground frame was brought into use is not known; in these instances, we quote the date of the relevant Board of Trade inspection report - in some cases, the BoT inspection was retrospective

Name	Opened	Closed	Type; frame	Notes
Tees Valley Junction	BoT report 1.5.1868			
Cotherstone	by 5.1898			
Scotts Siding GF	BoT report 13.11.1884		Ground frome; 6 levers	Contractor's siding - construction of Hury Reservoir
Scotts Siding GF	BoT report 29.11.1893	c.1896	Ground frame; 7 levers	Contractor's siding - construction of Blackton Reservoir
Romaldkirk Goods Yard GF	by 1907			Key kept at station
Romaldkirk				South of level crossing
Micketon Quarry (1)	BoT report 5.5.1873	8.1891 ?		
Mickelton Quarry (2)	BoT report 20.8.91		Cabin; 10 levers	
Mickleton GF			In station buildings	Locked by padlock; key kept at station office
Grassholme Reservoir Siding GF	BoT report 15.2.1901	c.1914	Dwarf frame; 7 levers	Contractor's siding - construction of Grassholme Reservoir
Lunedale Quarry Siding GF	BoT report 1.5.1878	c.1922	Ground frame with key	Lunedale Whinstone Co siding - 1m 77yds from Mickleton station
Hodsman Siding GF	c.1917 *		Ground frame; 3 levers	Electrically controlled from Middleton box * BoT inspection report dated 12.11.1925
Middleton-in-Teesdale	BoT report 5.8.1884		26 levers	BoT report dated 12.11.1925 refers to 35-lever box (28 in use, 7 spare)
Middleton Station GF	in 1.3.1922 WTT appendix		Ground frame	275yds west of signal box

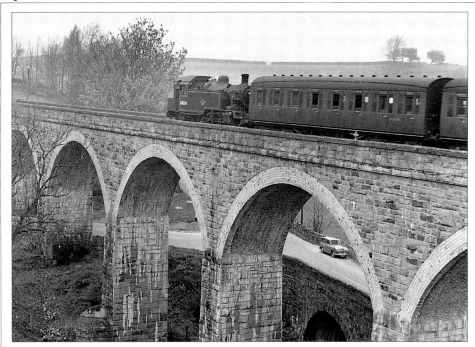

The Middleton-in-Teesdale branch crossed the River Lune by means of a sturdy five-arch stone-built viaduct. On a lower level, the B6277 Barnard Castle-Middleton road crossed the river on another bridge - the Hillman estate car is parked on that road. This picture was taken in April 1957 when brand new Class 2 2-6-2T No.84024 was undertaking running-in turns on the branch. PHOTOGRAPH: J.W.ARMSTRONG TRUST

one of the walls of the viaduct had started to bulge; the Tees Valley company looked to the relatively inexpensive solution of using a pair of tie rods to secure the masonry, but the NER's engineers weren't too keen on this idea. They reported on 3 July 1876 that: '...the cost of putting in tie-rods and cast iron washers would not, we believe, prove more economical than taking down and rebuilding that portion of the masonry which is defective. The bulging out of the wall does not extend to more than 4 feet below the coping, and in repairing the damage there need be no interruption to the traffic'. On 19 February 1881 the NER engineers reported that the repairs to Balder Viaduct had proved satisfactory, but they urged the Tees Valley company to attend to other defective portions of the structure. One particular problem was that: '...the telegraph wires are fixed to the coping on the concave side of the bridge and the strain upon

them is so great that the stone on which they are fixed has been pulled forward and shows a tendency to move forward the upper courses of the masonry immediately underneath it. This should be remedied by attaching the wires to the coping on the convex side of the bridge'.

Resuming our journey along the line, after crossing the Balder the railway twisted sharply, giving splendid views northwards towards the village of Eggleston and, behind it, the expanse of Woodland Fell (somewhat misguidingly named, for it is bereft of trees). The next village along the route of the railway was Romaldkirk. The village dates back to Saxon times, and has often been described as one of the most attractive in Northern England; its houses are grouped around three greens, at the centre of which is the church of St.Romald, the home of an effigy of a knight who died in battle in 1304. But enough of the tourist guide... **Romaldkirk** station (5m 27ch) did not open with the line in May 1868 - the railway company had considered that, because of the high price asked by the local landowners, the cost of a constructing station there would be too expensive. However, it was not too long before the station was provided; although the precise opening date seems to have gone unrecorded (somewhat mysteriously, there seems to be no record of a Board of Trade inspection - this should have been essential), Romaldkirk station made its first appearance in Bradshaws in July 1868. The station had a single platform with a simple, but attractive, stone building; at the south end of the platform the railway crossed a minor road on the level. Romaldkirk was actually a block post - this was simply to reduce the length of the block section thereby permitting trains

A splendid view of Middleton-in-Teesdale terminus in the early 1930s. D3 class 4-4-0 No.4354, a former Great Northern engine, prepares to depart for Barnard Castle; note the cattle truck at the front of the train. No.4354 was the first of four D3s to be fitted with side-window cabs in 1935 - this was after repeated requests by engine crews for additional protection, as their duties included the notoriously exposed Stainmore Line. This picture also provides a rare view of the Middleton turntable, which was taken out in the 1940s, and the original water tank. The wooden assembly in the left foreground is part of Ord & Maddison's loading dock. One other item of interest - note the lorry in the goods yard behind the station platform. PHOTOGRAPH: J.W.ARMSTRONG TRUST

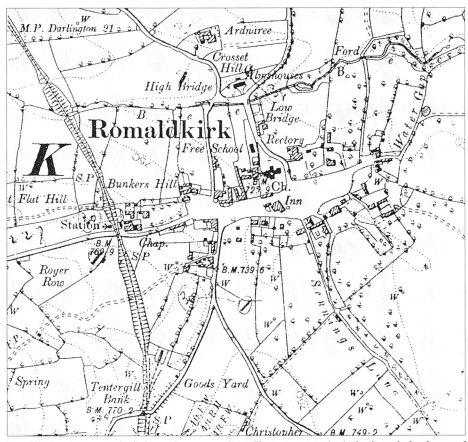

Romaldkirk - enlargement of 6" Ordnance Survey map of 1895. The passenger station is clearly marked to the west of the village, but note the goods yard, a completely separate entity beyond the south-west end of the village. CROWN COPYRIGHT

travelling in the same direction to follow one another more closely. The signal box was to the south of the level crossing.

There were no goods facilities at Romaldkirk station itself, the goods yard being almost ½-mile to the south, alongside the Hunderthwaite Lane bridge. The goods yard comprised only three sidings and had modest facilities. It appears that the warehouse, at least, had been constructed, not by the railway company, but by one of its customers - the minutes of a meeting of the Tees Valley Railway directors on 28 April 1869 refer to 'Facilities at Romaldkirk for the produce of the London Lead Company', noting that it had been proposed by Mr.R.W.Dainbridge that the lead company (whom he represented) should undertake '...the needful earth work and build the wall and supply the entrance and outlet doors...' for the goods facilities at Romaldkirk, with the proviso that the facilities be devoted exclusively to the lead company. The Tees Valley directors agreed, '...but with the understanding that they are not debarred from sending a reasonable proportion by Haggerleazes (near Butterknowle)...'. Clearly, an agreement was not imminent, as in 1873 the two daily goods trains on the branch ran non-stop to

and from Middleton-in-Teesdale - in other words, there was nothing for them to do at Romaldkirk. Nevertheless, facilities - including a warehouse - were eventually provided, and in later years the warehouse was used by Teesdale Associated Farmers. The railway continued from Romaldkirk in a generally north-westerly direction, climbing at a slightly easier 1 in 149. On the west side of the line about a mile and a half after leaving Romaldkirk, a siding diverged to Mickleton Quarry. The works were discussed by the Tees Valley Railway's directors on 13 February 1873: '...sidings have been laid and signals are being erected. The work was performed by the railway company's platelayers; the time they have been engaged on this work beyond the railway company's boundary has been carefully kept, and the limestone company will be charged with the value of the work...'. A signal cabin controlling the points and signals was inspected on 5 May 1873. It appears that another new junction was laid in 1891 - by this time Mickleton Quarry was owned by the Cargo Fleet Iron Company, whose private siding agreement was dated 14 July 1891. A new signal box containing 10 levers (9 in use, 1 spare) was installed; when inspecting the new arrangements for the Board of Trade, Major-General Hutchinson (as he then was) noted that '...on account of the falling gradient towards Barnard Castle, it is intended to work the siding by up (i.e. southbound) trains only'.

The last of the three intermediate stations was **Mickleton** (7m 8ch) which, in common with the other two stations, comprised a single platform and a modest, single-story building. A ground frame was accommodated in the station buildings, the key to unlock the frame being kept in the station office. The station was 826ft above sea level, and was the highest point of the branch. Just under ½-mile to the north of Mickleton, sidings were installed on the west side of the line in 1900 for use by the contractor, J.Scott, who was engaged on the construction of Grassholme Reservoir. A ground frame containing seven levers was provided at the point where J.Scott's siding joined the branch. The siding was disconnected from the branch line in 1914 after the reservoir had been completed, but a two-mile section of the siding remained in situ on the bed of the reservoir. At the point where the siding connected with the branch line, the latter was on a falling gradient towards Middleton-in-Teesdale; the siding connection faced downhill, and so the railway company had to give a formal undertaking to the Board of Trade that any movements into and out of the siding would be performed with the locomotive at the lower end (i.e. the Middleton-in-Teesdale end). The obligatory Board of Trade inspection of the siding connections in 1901 was conducted by Lt-Col.P.G.von Donop, who had at least two claims to fame - the first being he was the godfather of P.G.Wodehouse (and shared the same forenames, Pelham Grenville), the second being that he had almost indecipherable handwriting. On the latter count, it is conspicuous that the first Board of Trade reports to be typewritten were those of Lt-Col von Donop - clearly, the BoT were aware

A8 4-6-2T No.69856, a West Auckland engine, stands at Middleton-in-Teesdale station with a train for Bishop Auckland and Durham some time in the mid-1950s. The turntable has been removed, and the old water tank treated to a coat of paint. The A8s first came to the branch in 1938 after the lifting of restrictions. PHOTOGRAPH: J.W.ARMSTRONG TRUST

of the difficulties with his hand-written reports! But we digress...

Continuing northwards, the railway crossed the River Lune by means of sturdy stone-built viaduct which had five arches, each of 50ft span, and a maximum height of 60ft. Similarly to the Balder Viaduct, the Lune Viaduct is stated to have cost 'a little under £5,000' to construct. Just beyond the northern end of the viaduct was a siding to deal with traffic from Greengates Quarry belonging to the Lunedale Whinstone Company; the siding was connected to the branch line (the connection was facing Middleton-in-Teesdale), the arrangements being inspected for the Board of Trade in April 1878. It is believed that the ground frame controlling the siding connection was taken out of use shortly after World War I, though it wasn't deleted from railway company records until 1923. The stone from Greengates Quarry was brought to the siding by means of a 2ft 6in gauge railway; over the years, three differ-

ent locomotives were used on the narrow gauge system - a Black Hawthorn 0-4-0ST of 1882 and two Bagnall 0-4-0STs, one of 1887 and the other of 1910. All three had been purchased new by the whinstone company and, when the second and third arrived on site, the engine shed had to be extended on both occasions.

Lunedale Quarry was later acquired by George Hodsmans & Sons who installed a new siding 275 yards closer to Middleton-in-Teesdale, the siding agreement being dated 2 April 1917. The siding and its connections were retrospectively inspected for the Ministry of Transport in November 1925 (see accompanying document).

Continuing northwards, the Tees Valley branch was on a steady 1 in 200 ascent towards the terminus at **Middleton-in-Teesdale** (8m 61ch from Barnard Castle station). The station originally appeared in the timetables simply as Middleton, the 'in Teesdale' suffix not appearing until the June 1894 timetables. The station was

786ft above sea level on the south-west bank of the River Tees; the Tees used to mark the boundary between Yorkshire and County Durham, and so Middleton-in-Teesdale station - and, for that matter, the entire length of the Tees Valley Railway - was on the Yorkshire side of the river. But although Middleton-in-Teesdale station was in Yorkshire, the actual town was on the north-east bank of the Tees in County Durham.

Near the station platform were an engine shed and turntable. It is unclear what, if any, accommodation was originally provided for the branch locomotive at the terminus, as the Tees Valley company's minute books for 2 January 1869 (almost eight months after the line had opened) refer to: '...an estimate of £194.19.4 for the erection of an engine shed at Middleton-in-Teesdale'. As an alternative to having a new shed constructed, the Tees Valley noted that there was a suitable building available at Shildon and asked the NER for a quote for its removal and reassembly at Middleton. Nothing came of that proposal, and so further tenders were obtained for the construction of an engine shed at Middleton-in-Teesdale. The job was given to Mr. Hepworth for a fee of £196, and the shed was presumably opened later in 1869. The turntable at Middleton was taken out in the 1940s, presumably a consequence of the introduction of push-pull workings.

There were several sidings in the yard at Middleton-in-Teesdale; on the west side of the yard were connections to Ord & Maddison's siding - this siding extended for a distance of a couple of miles northwards along Teesdale to Crossthwaite Quarries. The quarry company was one of the Tees Valley Railway's principal customers, and became famous in industrial railway circles in later years for a pair of ex-NER 0-4-0Ts (LNER Y7 class Nos. 898 and 1302) which had been purchased for £250 each in 1929/30. The Y7s were used to bring the stone from the quarries to the washing plant in the station yard at Middleton-in-Teesdale and, of course, to take empty wagons back to the quarry. On the final trip of the day - around 5.00pm - a van was added at the rear of the train to take the quarrymen home from work; the van was uncoupled and left at the station overnight. The Y7s were used at the quarry until the internal railway was dismantled in 1952, and they were both scrapped on site in 1952/53. In earlier times Ord & Maddison had had a third

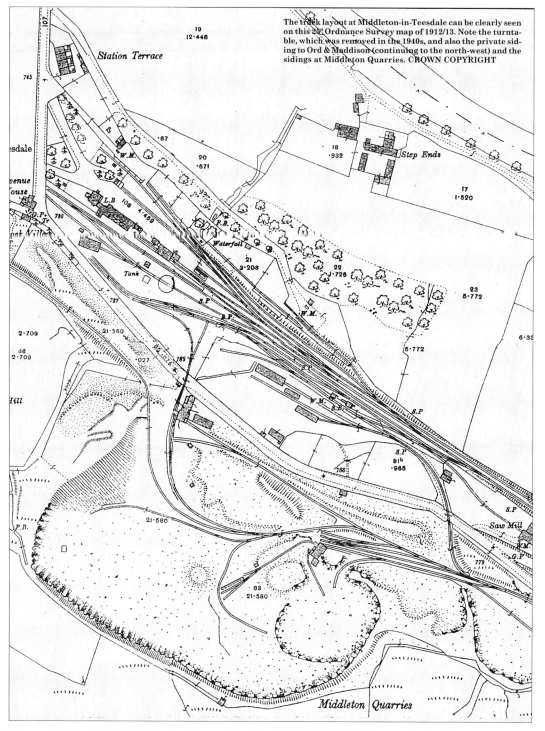

The track layout at Middleton-in-Teesdale can be clearly seen on this 25" Ordnance Survey map of 1912/13. Note the turntable, which was removed in the 1940s, and also the private siding to Ord & Maddison (continuing to the north-west) and the sidings at Middleton Quarries. CROWN COPYRIGHT

locomotive - this was an outside cylinder 0-4-0ST which carried the works plate of T.D.Ridley & Sons, Middlesbrough, a firm which was once described as a 'well-known locomotive bodger and repairer', and was 'quite capable of disguising a locomotive's origins'.

At Middleton-in-Teesdale station, the siding accommodation was extended on at least two occasions to keep pace with an increase in stone traffic. The first major alterations were completed in 1884, the works being described as '...an improvement of the platform, additional siding accommodation, the rearrangement of the existing sidings, and the concentration and interlocking of the points and signal levers in a new raised cabin containing 26 levers'. By 1925 the signal box frame had been extended to 35 levers, of which 28 were in use. The station itself had only ever had a single platform. During the winter it was rather exposed, but regular users of the line used to congregate in the porters' room which, with its hearty fire, was somewhat more hospitable.

Jumping ahead to 1938, the LNER's *Handbook of Stations* listed the following tenants at Middleton-in-Teesdale station:
• Harwood Mining Company (siding between Mickleton and Middleton)
• Hodsman & Sons
• Middleton Saw Mill & Timber Yard
• Ord & Maddison (quarry proprietors)
• Park End Quarries

Top. When it came to delightfully rural branch line termini, Middleton-in-Teesdale took some beating! This view of the station yard was taken from the B6277 road in Spring 1957; the rear wall of the engine shed shows evidence of alteration or repair - given that there was never a track running through the shed, could it be that a locomotive had once collided with the rear wall, thereby necessitating substantial repairs? Also evident is the newer water tank (on the timber framing) - when this was brought into use, the stone building under the old tank (seen more clearly in other pictures) was given over to the platelayers for use as a cabin and stores. Between the old and new water tanks is Sunderland-based A8 4-6-2T No.69857.

Middle. Middleton-in-Teesdale station, this time on a rather damp 25 October 1952, with a push-pull set at the platform. On the extreme left, the engine shed is visible beyond the new water tank. The space in the foreground was once occupied by the turntable. PHOTOGRAPH: J.W.ARMSTRONG TRUST

Bottom. For working the private railway between their quarries and the yard at Middleton-in-Teesdale station, Messrs.Ord & Maddison purchased two Y9 class 0-4-0Ts from the LNER in 1929/30. The first of the pair was LNER No.898, which had been built for the North Eastern Railway in 1888. Along with its sister engine, ex-LNER No.1302, it remained on site until 1952, having assisted - somewhat insultingly, perhaps - in the lifting of the track on which it had spent the last thirty-odd years of its working life. This picture was taken near Middleton on 25 October 1952, not long before the locomotive was cut up. PHOTOGRAPH: J.W.ARMSTRONG TRUST

The delights of Middleton-in-Teesdale, population 1,657, as listed in the *AA Touring Gazeteer* for 1946.

In business

Going back to the early days of the Tees Valley Railway, as had been originally intended it was worked from by the North Eastern Railway who provided the locomotives and rolling stock. It appears that the NER took only 30% of receipts for 'working expenses' - this was a very low percentage, the usual 'cut' for a working company in those days being in the region of 50%. As will be seen in the accompanying table, the services on the line initially comprised three passenger trains each way on weekdays; after completing its first return trip of the day, the branch engine worked the daily goods train from Middleton-in-Teesdale at 9.30am, returning from Barnard Castle at 10.40am. However, by 1870, if not before, the outgoing goods train on Wednesdays - market day - had been reorganised to run as a mixed train, leaving Middleton-in-Teesdale at 9.15am. Later, the mixed train was replaced by an ordinary passenger train, albeit at a slightly earlier time.

The first and last branch trains of the day started and terminated at Middleton-in-Teesdale, and so the branch engine was accommodated in the engine shed there overnight. This was the usual practice for almost all of the eighty-eight years for which steam haulage prevailed on the line.

Unusually, trains from Barnard Castle to Middleton-in-Teesdale were regarded as going in the 'up' direction - the widely accepted practice was for trains heading in the general direction of London to be regarded as 'up' - though by the 1890s the 'direction' on the Tees Valley line had been regularised, with 'up' meaning towards Barnard Castle.

The Tees Valley Railway quickly settled down to a fairly routine existence. The stone traffic, in particular, soon provided a steady flow of traffic, but it was still necessary for a close watch to be kept on the pennies. For example, at a meeting of the Tees Valley directors on 7 November 1868: *'...the question of revising the staffing was gone into with a view to it being reduced if possible. It was considered that Mr.Gibson, the Station Master at Middleton, might do the whole of the work there, and thus do away with two clerks. It was also considered that one Porter would do all the work connected with the Passenger Station and Goods Warehouse'.* And at the same meeting: *'With regard to the payment by this company for the Omnibus between the Middleton Station and High Force, it was resolved that, as the season is now advanced, this be discontinued'.*

In 1871 the Cumberland & Cleveland Junction Railway was formed to promote an extension from Middleton-in-Teesdale to Alston -

this extension had been in the mind of the Tees Valley directors from the outset. However, no capital was forthcoming and so the Cumberland & Cleveland scheme passed into oblivion.

The stone traffic continued to develop, but the NER considered that there could have been greater development. In a letter to the Tees Valley directors on 13 February 1873, it was opined that: *'...further extension of the sidings at Middleton-in-Teesdale is absolutely necessary to work the increasing traffic at this place. During the*

MINISTRY OF TRANSPORT,
7, Whitehall Gardens,
London, S.W.1.

17th November, 1925.

SIR,

I have the honour to report, for the information of the Minister of Transport, that I made an Inspection on the 12th instant of the new work at Middleton-in-Teesdale, on the Tees Valley Branch of the London and North Eastern Railway.

This work consists of a new connection in the single line east of the station, to a siding constructed for Messrs. G. Hodsman & Son, facing traffic in the direction of Middleton.

This siding connection is situated within the signal area controlled from Middleton Station box, from which it is distant 507 yards. The connection is worked from a three-lever ground frame, which is electrically controlled from the station box, one of these levers being in connection with this release and the other two working respectively the plunger and the points. The station signal box contains 28 working and 7 spare levers, and the interlocking at the ground frame and that between this frame and the box is correct.

A few yards east of the new connection is situated No. 35 down home signal, 70 yards east of which is situated No. 5 up advance starting signal. The length of single line between these two signals has been track circuited with an indicator in the station box. It would in my opinion have been preferable for No. 35 down home signal to have been moved to some convenient position east of No. 5 up advance starting signal and the track circuit laid as a train waiting indication east of the former. I do not however consider that in the circumstances such an alteration need be called for, but it would be advisable for the existing track circuit and also No. 25 release lever in the station signal box to control the block working to Mickleton.

The arrangements otherwise are satisfactory, and subject to the addition of this or some other acceptable control, I recommend that this work be approved.

I have the honour to be, Sir,
Your obedient Servant,

(Sgd.) G.L.Hall,
Major.

Above. The Ministry of Transport inspection report of the connections to Hodsman's Siding at Middleton-in-Teesdale, 19 November 1925.

Middleton-in-Teesdale engine shed, 1 September 1956. PHOTOGRAPH: T.J.EDGINGTON

G5 0-4-4T No.67273 stands with its push-pull set at Middleton-in-Teesdale on 25 October 1952. PHOTOGRAPH: J.W.ARMSTRONG TRUST

TEES VALLEY RAILWAY.

REGULATIONS

FOR WORKING THE TEES VALLEY LINE BETWEEN BARNARD CASTLE AND MIDDLETON.

GENERAL INSTRUCTIONS.

The Line is to be worked by what is designated the "Train Staff" mode of working.

Either a Train Staff or a Train Ticket is to be carried with each Engine or Train to and fro, and no Engine or Train is to be allowed to start without one of these.

The Line will be worked in one Section, and one Staff will be employed between ~~Barnard Castle~~ *The Tees Valley Junction* and Middleton, coloured Blue. *and the Trains between the Teesdale Junction and Barnard Castle Station will be worked by a pilot man. L Railton sec[y]*

No Engine or Train is to be permitted to leave Barnard Castle or Middleton unless the Staff is at the Station.

If no other Engine or Train is intended to follow, the Staff is to be given to the Guard or person in charge.

If another Engine or Train is intended to follow, before the Staff can be returned, a Train Ticket will be given to the person in charge of the leading Train, the Staff itself being given to the person in charge of the last Train, after which no Engine or Train can leave the Station under any circumstances whatever, until the Staff is returned.

The Train Tickets are to be kept in charge of the Station Master at Barnard Castle and Middleton.

The *Train Tickets* and *Ticket Boxes* are to be of the same colour as the Staff to which they apply.

A Guard or Engineman, taking a Staff or Ticket beyond the portion of line to which it belongs, or leaving a Station without the Staff or Ticket, as hereinbefore explained, will render himself liable to dismissal (although no accident may arise).

No Engineman is to start from either Station until the *person in charge* of his Train has shown him the Train Staff or Ticket.

The usual Special Train Signals are to be used for the guidance of the Gatekeepers and Platelayers. A Red Board or Flag by day, or an additional lighted Red Tail Lamp placed on the Train or Engine by night, denotes that another Train or Engine is following.

Ballast Trains are to be treated in every respect like Traffic Trains as regards the Staff and Ticket arrangements.

In the event of an Engine or Train breaking down between two Stations, the Fireman is to take the Train Staff to the Station in the direction whence assistance may be expected, that the Staff may be at the Station on the arrival of an Engine. Should the Engine that fails be in possession of a Train Ticket, instead of the Staff, assistance can only come from the Station at which the Train Staff has been left.

The Fireman must, in such a case, procure a "Red Flag" by day, or "hand Signal Lamp" by night, and return to the nearest Telegraph Station, or until he meets an Engine or Train with the Train Staff, taking care to place an Explosive Signal on the rails at a distance of 400 yards from the disabled Train, and Two such Signals when at a distance of 800 yards.

All parties concerned in the carrying out of these Regulations are expected, not only strictly to adhere to them, but also to report any infringement they may observe by others.

LANC. RAILTON,

Secretary.

The Tees Valley Railway's draft working instructions for the Middleton branch, April 1868. Lancelot Railton's handwritten notes were, of course, added to the final draft.

three months ending December, 7,535 tons of stone were sent out of Ord & Maddison's works (an average approximately 10 wagons per working day), *and this would have been largely increased if greater facilities for getting it out had been afforded. The siding at the west end requires 67 additional yards, and at the east end 50 yards. A crane is also very much wanted for the goods siding, as at present there are no means for unloading heavy casks etc except by gathering up all the men who can be found round about, which is very unsatisfactory'.*

The NER, as the working company, kept a close, but rather paternal, eye on the Tees Valley, undertaking regular inspections and following up with a report and recommendations. One such report was prepared on 21 February 1873: *'...the earthworks and masonry have weathered the late severe season in a most satisfactory manner. Of the condition of the permanent way we cannot however speak so favourably. The 500 new sleepers, which we understood were ordered some time ago, have not yet come to hand, and in many places the line is getting into bad repair for want of them, and will soon be really dangerous to passenger traffic. Including the abovementioned quantity we now require 1200 new sleepers for renewals in the main line, and no time should be lost in getting them in, or we are afraid that some accident will result. We recommend that, if possible, these sleepers should be got from the Stockton & Darlington Company, as they creosote them at their own works, and they are much better done than any which are got from the merchants. Some of the permanent rails are showing considerable signs of wear, and about 100 of them have already been turned.*

The passenger platforms require a coat of gravel, or black ballast. The latter would be the cheaper but the Station Masters complain of it being treaded into the waiting rooms and offices.

Romaldkirk - there is a want of accommodation for cattle traffic at the station. A cattle pen might be erected on the present loading bank at a cost of £5. The Station Master also asks for a platform for heavy goods, which he says have at present to be lifted with the carts at the expense of truck time and labour. The cost of such a platform would be about £12. There is no name up at the Romaldkirk passenger station*, and, as we understand that passengers for this place have occasionally passed beyond the station, it would be desirable to have a name-board put up similar to those at the other stations. (* The lack of a nameboard at Romaldkirk station was highly irregular, as a nameboard was normally insisted on by the Board of Trade; but, given that no BoT inspection report for Romaldkirk station has come to light, could it possibly be that the station was not actually inspected? - *Ed*).

Middleton-in-Teesdale - we have examined the proposed extension of siding accommodation required by Messrs.Ord & Maddison...we estimate the cost of material and labour for the additional 117 yards of sidings at £100. With reference to a crane at the station, we think that a second-hand one may be obtained from the Stockton & Darlington Company. (The NER engineers seemed rather adept at finding buyers for old S&D materials and equipment). We have received a letter from the London Lead Company asking for more depot room at the station. We estimate the cost of 2 new depots, including permanent way, at about £120....we suggest that the Lead Company should pay some rent, or at least an acknowledgement to the Tees Valley Company otherwise they will obtain a right to the ground they are now occupying, which would seriously prejudice this company (the NER) in the event of the land in question being required, as it may be before very long, for increased traffic accommodation'.

The working timetable for July 1873 shows that there were now two scheduled return goods trains each weekday:

• 10.13am ex-Barnard Castle; 12.05pm ex-Middleton-in-Teesdale (listed as 'goods and minerals')
• 1.15pm ex-Barnard Castle; 4.55pm ex-Middleton-in-Teesdale

Both were scheduled to run non-stop between Barnard Castle and Middleton-in-Teesdale; this suggests that the first of the rail-connected quarries along the line - Mickleton Quarry - had not yet started to dispatch stone by rail. It also suggests that the goods facilities at Cotherstone and Romaldkirk were not yet fully in operation, despite the latter having been the subject of correspondence in 1869 and again in 1872.

In their report dated 25 January 1875, the NER's engineers noted the usual requirements for a supply of permanent way materials - replacement rails, chairs, sleepers etc etc - but added that replacement rails weighing 75lb to the yard had already started to be laid at certain places to replace the original 55lb rails. The engineers also noted: *'The traffic at Middleton Station is increasing so much that it will be necessary to provide a new goods siding as soon as possible. Iron rails and chairs for this can be obtained from the main line as soon as new rails are provided and laid in. The question of additional waiting room accommodation at Middleton is also pressing for attention, and a Porters' room, available for lamps and parcels, seems also desirable'.*

On 3 July 1876 the engineers opined that: *'...the signals on the whole of the line require painting, and also the woodwork of Romaldkirk station; the ceiling and walls in the waiting room and booking offices there also require attention'.*

Unlike several of its contemporaries, the Tees Valley Railway received a reasonably steady income from its working company. Passenger traffic figures for two random months are:

August 1880:
First class - 184
Second class - 199

'Government' - 8,415
Total - 8,799
Total revenue - £209.3.8½d
Parcels traffic - £11.7.8d
TVR proportion - £159.19.5d

January 1882:
First class - 101
Second class - 139
'Government' - 4,752
Total - 4,992
Total revenue - £106.9.3d
Parcels traffic - £5.19.9d
TVR proportion - £80.2.3d

The foregoing were fairly typical figures for the period in that they showed a significant increase in traffic during the summer months. Clearly, the scenic delights of Teesdale during the summer period were widely known and well appreciated even in those days.

Despite the above figures - which were better than those of some other small, localised railway companies - the Tees Valley Railway found itself in debt. The inevitable solution was a sell-out to the North Eastern Railway - this was agreed in 1880 but was not ratified until 19 June 1882. The NER, which by this time already had a £31,000 share of Tees Valley capital, agreed to buy out the other TVR shareholders for £25,188 and discharge a debt of some £22,000. These terms gave the TVR's shareholders a return of £19.7.6 for each £25 share.

North Eastern days

By the early 1890s there were six passenger trains each way on the branch on weekdays; the goods and mineral traffic had continued to increase, and now warranted three trains each weekday. For a period in the early 1890s the engine shed at Middleton-in-Teesdale was closed and the engine for the first branch train of the day (6.45am ex-Middleton) ran light from Barnard Castle; similarly, the engine off the last train (arrive Middleton 9.35pm) returned light to Barnard Castle.

The building of Hury and Blackton Reservoirs in Baldersdale between 1884 and 1896 bought considerable construction traffic to the line. As noted earlier, the contractor, W.Scott, had his own siding north of Cotherstone where traffic could be loaded and unloaded. The construction of Grassholme Reservoir between 1901 and 1914 also brought additional traffic to the line.

The general pattern of branch services changed considerably in the period prior to World War I. One of the major changes was that the branch trains no longer worked exclusively between Middleton-in-Teesdale and Barnard Castle - of the up trains, three each day worked through to Bishop Auckland, one to Sunderland and one to South Shields, while of the down trains, one worked through from Bishop Auckland and one from Leamside. On Saturdays, there was a summertime excursion from Saltburn to Middleton-in-Teesdale (arrive at Middleton 3.09pm, depart 8.05pm). There was also a Sunday service on the branch:

• 9.35am ex-Barnard Castle; engine returned light from Middleton-in-Teesdale
• 5.35pm ex-Middleton-in-Teesdale; engine for this train sent out light from

On 29 July 1957 G5 No.67258 prepares to leave Middleton-in-Teesdale with the 11.40am to Durham. This was the last summer of regular steam working on the Middleton-in-Teesdale branch; for the start of that year's winter timetable, DMUs took over. **PHOTOGRAPH: IAN S.CARR**

The end of the road - the *very* end. G5 No.67258 prepares to run round its train at Middleton-in-Teesdale on 24 July 1957. Although the G5s had become established on push-pull workings on the Middleton branch, the need for running round in this instance confirms that this particular train was not operating as a push-pull. The engine had arrived with the 8.23am from Sunderland, which it had taken over at Durham; this train wasn't a through working from Sunderland in the true sense, as it had a 32-minute wait at Barnard Castle in order to connect with the 10.00am Darlington-Penrith. The wait at Barnard Castle was spent in the 'west end bay'. PHOTOGRAPH: IAN S.CARR

Barnard Castle

After World War I, the Sunday trains ran through to and from Darlington.

Two sets of engine crews were based at Middleton-in-Teesdale at this time.

The passenger train loadings for the Middleton-in-Teesdale branch during NER days were 170 tons for a train hauled by a 2-4-0 and comprised of bogie carriages (this was equivalent to seven carriages) or 153 tons for a train of six-wheeled carriages (equivalent to twelve).

Post-grouping

In 1923, the Tees Valley line became part of the London & North Eastern Railway. Until the mid-1920s the motive power usually took the form of ex-NER '901' or '1463' class 2-4-0s (who said 7ft driving wheels were unsuitable for a branch line with gradients of up to 1 in 85!), but in 1925 D23 class 4-4-0 No.217 became the regular branch engine, being allocated to Middleton-in-Teesdale shed. Following No.217's transfer to Barnard Castle in December 1930, some hitherto 'foreign' locomotives started to appear on the line. Those which were allocated to Middleton-in-Teesdale were:
• Ex-Hull & Barnsley (LNER J23 class) 0-6-0 No.2514; December 1930 to June 1931 - replaced briefly at Middleton by former regular D23 No.217
• Ex-Great Northern (LNER D3 class) 4-4-0 No.4354; August 1931 to July 1936 (other members of the class, including No.4347, are known to have been used on the Middleton branch in the mid-1930s)

• Ex-Great Eastern (LNER E4 class) 2-4-0 No.7416; according to official records the allocation was from July 1936 to July 1938, but it is known that the engine was replaced at Middleton prior to July 1938 by a V1 2-6-2T
• A8 class 4-6-2T No.1524; July 1938 to March 1939 (the A8s had hitherto been prohibited from the Middleton branch)
• A8 No.1525; March 1939 to May 1939
• A8 No.1766; May 1939 to September 1939.

However, given that an increasing number of branch workings ran through to or from places such as Darlington and Durham, it was unsurprising that other locomotives were seen at Middleton. And it wasn't only locomotives. During much of the 1930s it was usual to see one or even two of the LNER's Sentinel-Cammell railcars on the branch each weekday. By mid-1932 a Shildon railcar was diagrammed to work the 10.25am Bishop Auckland to Middleton-in-Teesdale service and the corresponding return trip. Shildon shed closed in July 1935, and many of its duties passed, in some form or other, to West Auckland shed, which had just been reopened after being mothballed for four years. The West Auckland diagrams for July 1935 included a Sentinel railcar working ('Car 1') on the 8.40am Darlington-Middleton and 10.10am return, and another working ('Car 2') on the 3.27pm Sunderland-Middleton and 6.00pm return to Bishop Auckland. At the time, West Auckland had five Sentinel railcars to cover three diagrams; the cars were all six-cylinder versions: No.2136 HOPE, No.2144 TRAVELLER, No.2152 COURRIER, No.2218 TELEGRAPH and No.2261 DILIGENCE.

In 1937/38, a Tyne Dock railcar had a daily trip from South Shields to Middleton-in-Teesdale, albeit as three separate workings - it left South Shields at 4.06pm for Durham, then worked the 5.27pm to Barnard Castle; it waited for over an hour at Barnard Castle, standing in the bay platform at the west end of the station, before proceeding to Middleton-

On 23 July 1957, G5 No.67320 awaits departure from Middleton-in-Teesdale for Bishop Auckland. Note the first class accommodation in the leading coach. PHOTOGRAPH: IAN S.CARR

MIDDLETON-IN-TEESDALE and BARNARD CASTLE—Weekdays.

Distance from Middleton-in-Teesdale (M.C.)	UP.	1 PASSENGER a.m.	2 PASSENGER a.m.	3 PASSENGER (G) a.m.	4 Goods (D) (WO) a.m.	6 PASSENGER (B) p.m.	8 Goods (C) (Q) p.m.	9 PASSENGER arr.	9 PASSENGER dep. p.m.	Sundays — Light Engine 1 a.m.	Sundays — PASSENGER 2 arr.	Sundays — PASSENGER 2 dep. p.m.
	Middleton-in-Teesdale † dep.	6 46	8 16	9 36	10 30	2 10	4 10	—	5 35	10 10	—	5 35
1 53	Mickleton	6 50	8 20	9 40	10 42	2 14	..	—	5 39	–	—	5 39
3 34	Romaldkirk	6 55	8 25	9 46	11 1	2 19	..	5 44	5 46	..	5 44	5 46
5 73	Cotherstone	7 0	8 30	9 52	11 18	2 24	..	5 51	5 53	..	5 51	5 53
7 55	*Tees Valley Junction* †	7 3	8 33	9 55	11 24	2 27	..		5 56	10 22	5 56	
8 61	**Barnard Castle** arr.	7 6	8 36	9 58	11 28	2 30	4 44	6 1	6 16	10 25	5 59	6 5
	Arrives at destination	Bishop Auckl'nd 7.43 a.m. (p.252)	Durham 9.41 a.m. (p.252)		North Road 12.45 p.m. (p.260)	North Road 3.15 p.m. (p.252)	North Road 6.0 p.m. (p.261)	Durham 7.23 p.m. (p.262)			Darlington 6.47 p.m. (p.261)	

B—To work all road traffic to and from stations and sidings on the branch. Auckland direction. † Bay Platform. G—Horse boxes and carriage trucks will not be conveyed except for Bishop

BARNARD CASTLE and MIDDLETON-IN-TEESDALE—Weekdays.

Distance from Barnard Castle (M.C.)	DOWN.	1 Goods (D) a.m.	2 PASSENGER arr. a.m.	2 PASSENGER dep. a.m.	4 PASSENGER a.m.	5 PASSENGER (WO) a.m.	7 Goods (C) (Q) p.m.	11 PASSENGER p.m.	13 PASSENGER p.m.	Sundays — PASSENGER 1 a.m.	Sundays — PASSENGER 2 p.m.
	Departs from	North Road 5.55 a.m. (p.258)	Leamside 5.50 a.m. (p.263)				North Road 1.15 p.m. (p.259)		Darlington 8.45 a.m. (p.259)		
	Barnard Castle dep.	7 0	7 25		7 41	9 0	1 36	4 49	6 30	9 35	5 5
1 5	*Tees Valley Junction* †	7 5	7	43	7 43	9 2	1 38	4 51	6 32	9 37	5 7
2 68	Cotherstone	A	7 47		7 49	9 7	1 43	4 56	6 37	9 42	....
5 27	Romaldkirk	....	7 54		7 56	9 13	1 49	5 2	6 43	9 48	..
7 8	Mickleton	....		8 1		9 18	1 54	5 7	6 48	9 53	..
8 61	**Middleton-in-Teesdale** † arr.	7 41	8 5	—		9 22	1 58 (3 5)	5 11	6 52	9 58	5 20

North Eastern Railway working timetable, 11 July 1921 u.f.n. Note the two goods trains on weekdays.

in-Teesdale where it arrived at 7.23pm. It departed from Middleton at 8.20pm with a through working to Sunderland.

The West Auckland rosters for September 1938 still included three Sentinel railcar diagrams, two of which took in trips to Middleton-in-Teesdale. The diagram for 'Car 1' included the 8.40am Darlington-Middleton and 10.10am return, while 'Car 3' covered the 3.27pm Sunderland-Middleton and 6.06pm return to Bishop Auckland. The five cars mentioned above all remained at West Auckland until the end of 1940. A trip in - or, rather, behind - one of them was recalled by Mr.John Aylard in the March 1978 issue of the *SLS Journal*: '...on a Saturday in August 1938 I had the unique experience of riding in a peculiar LNER vehicle which I had great difficulty in believing belonged to the same railway company which produced the *Silver Jubilee* and the 1938 *Flying Scotsman* sets. It was one of eight Clayton-built 4-wheeled railcar trailers and was hauled by 2144 TRAVELLER'.

In the summer of 1939 the Middleton-in-Teesdale branch was served by seven trains each way on weekdays with one additional working on Wednesdays and two on Saturdays. By this time almost of the trains ran through to or from Durham or Darlington, and the 4.08pm from Middleton to Darlington actually ran non-stop to Barnard Castle. On Sundays there were no less than six trains each way working through to and from Bishop Auckland,

Darlington, Newcastle or Saltburn.

In September 1939 the resident A8 at Middleton-in-Teesdale shed, No.1766, was replaced by G5 class 0-4-4T No.1764. The G5s had been introduced in 1894 and the class eventually comprised 110 locomotives; they were sturdy, economical and hugely versatile little engines, and apart from working in almost every nook and cranny in the north-east of England, some later gravitated to the old Great Eastern Section others to Scotland. No.1764 went on to enjoy a thirteen-year residency at Middleton, until June 1952 - it was renumbered 7309 in May 1946 and BR No.67309 in March 1951.

During World War II the branch continued to be served by six trains each way on weekdays, principally because a large number of troops were stationed in the area. For a while, there was a Sunday service comprising one through train to and from Darlington in the evening. In an article in the *SLS Journal*, Mr.J.G.Ragsdale remembered his days living at Middleton-in-Teesdale during the war: 'I attended Barnard Castle school as a day scholar and so I travelled the line daily, including Saturdays, during term time. During this period my morning train - the second one out - departed behind a G5 at varying times between 7.40 and 7.50am, the journey time for the 8½ miles being about 25 minutes. This train was destined for Bishop Auckland and Durham (always carrying a contingent of school children to

'Bishop') and was preceded into Barnard Castle station by the train from Kirkby Stephen, via Stainmore, to Darlington. It was the custom of the Darlington train, hauled by a J21 0-6-0, to run through Barnard Castle station and reverse into the bay platform at the east end and for our train to follow into the station 'proper' under the train shed. Occasionally the Darlington train would be late and we would be held at the signal box at Tees Valley Junction, just before the viaduct where the tablet was taken over. During the winter and spring terms the afternoons at school were taken up with playing games, and lessons recommenced at 3.45pm, continuing until 5.45pm when we dashed the mile from school to the station to catch the train at 6.10 or 6.15pm from 'Barney' to Middleton'.

The early evening train from Barnard Castle to Middleton-in-Teesdale - the train on which Mr.Ragsdale used to return home from school - ran through from Darlington. It was a regular turn for running in locomotives ex-works, and consequently brought A5, A6, A7 and A8 4-6-2Ts, new L1 2-6-4Ts, and V1 and V3 2-6-2Ts to Middleton-in-Teesdale. Rather more unusual visitors to Middleton-in-Teesdale during the war were V2 2-6-2s; they are stated to have made several appearances on the branch, on at least one occasion being piloted by an A5 4-6-2T and on another occasion by a J39 0-6-0.

It was occasionally necessary to provide a substitute engine at Middleton-in-Teesdale while the regular G5 was away for repair. The replacement was usually another G5 - No.408 (which was later renumbered 7342 and later No.67342) is known to have been at Middleton *circa* 1945/46. It was reported in the *SLS Journal* that its regular driver was a rather stout chap '...who was frequently to be seen in the cab of his engine, feet up, facing AWAY from the direction of travel and reading an old *News of the World* while the Fireman attended to both driving and firing!'.

During the latter part of the LNER period, the permitted passenger train loadings on the Middleton-in-Teesdale branch were 120 tons (equivalent to five 49ft bogies) for an E4 2-4-0, 135 tons (five 52ft bogies) for an unsuperheated J21 0-6-0, and 155 tons (seven 49ft or six 52ft bogies) for a superheated J21 0-6-0.

State ownership

For the first few yeas of the BR era, life continued largely unchanged on the Middleton-in-Teesdale branch with seven or eight passenger trains each way on week-

Connections between Middleton-in-Teesdale and Kings Cross, as given in the *ABC Railway Guide* for March 1939.

through to Darlington - usually warranted four twin-articulated coaches, hauled by an A5 4-6-2T.

There was an unusual manifestation at Middleton-in-Teesdale on Whit Monday (14 May) 1951 when V2 2-6-2 No.60801 of Heaton shed arrived with a half-day excursion from South Shields. Having started its journey at 11.24am and run via Sunderland, Durham and Bishop Auckland, the excursion train was scheduled to arrive at Middleton at 2.00pm. The train comprised eight corridor bogies and

days and three on Sundays, and with G5 0 - 4 - 4 T No.67309 (as it became) as the r e s i d e n t Middleton engine.

The military presence remained in the Barnard Castle and Middleton areas long after World War II. The various camps required the running of special trains from time to time, and also generated considerable bursts of traffic at weekends. In the early 1950s one particular S a t u r d a y s Only train - the 1 . 2 5 p m

was worked right through by a Heaton crew, albeit with a local pilotman on the footplate from Bishop Auckland onwards. Despite a 15mph speed limit between Romaldkirk and Middleton, due to the line being relaid with concrete sleepers, the train arrived at the terminus six minutes early. However, even with the engine right up to the buffers the end of the train was fouling the points at the east end of the station, but fortunately A8 4-6-2T No.69856 was present, having brought in the previous train, and so it was commandeered to pull the coaches far enough back along the line to enable the V2 to be released. The V2 waited then outside the engine shed while the coaches were placed on one of the goods sidings. The A8 and V2 then ran coupled together (the V2 leading, tender-first) back to West Auckland where the V2 could be turned prior to returning to Middleton in readiness for the return trip.

In June 1952 the regular Middleton-in-Teesdale engine, G5 0-4-4T No.67309, was transferred to Heaton. By this time Middleton shed had lost the autonomy which it had enjoyed for many years (under BR auspices it was a sub-shed of Darlington, 51A), and its engine was subsequently supplied, in the more customary 'parent to sub-shed' manner, by Darlington. The engine was usually another G5 or a J21 0-6-0.

Various economies were introduced on the branch in 1954. Cotherstone and Mickleton stations lost their facilities for handling public goods traffic (though there probably had been precious little such traffic for some time), and were reduced to the status of unstaffed halts.

During the 1950s a new quarry was opened up in Lunedale in connection with the construction of Selset Reservoir, at the

west end of Grassholme Reservoir. After the reservoir was completed Messrs.Watson, Sayer continued to work the quarry, sending their stone to Middleton-in-Teesdale to be put on to rail. For a while, it amounted to ten 20-ton hoppers each weekday.

A report of contemporary comings and goings on the Middleton-in-Teesdale branch during a two-week period in July 1956 appeared in the *Railway Observer* magazine. It was noted that '...no purely branch line passenger trains were run - trains worked through to and from Darlington, Bishop Auckland and Sunderland, although certain of the latter trains had prolonged waits at Barnard Castle, when they were shunted into a bay platform there. Passenger traffic was entirely in the hands of NER locomotives. The Darlington trains were push-and-pull sets and G5s Nos.67284 and 67305 monopolised this service. The locomotive working the last train to Middleton, the 9.00pm ex-Darlington, was accommodated in the small sub-shed at Middleton overnight and also at the weekend. Middleton-Bishop Auckland trains were sometimes worked by G5s - Nos.67298 and 67343 were observed - but more usually by A8s - Nos.69851, 69852, 69856, 69857, 69863, 69872, 69874 and 69875 were all noted. The only blot on the pre-grouping landscape was the daily goods on which were seen Class 2 2-6-0s Nos.46476 and 46479 and Class 3 No.77004'.

The practice of using the Middleton-in-Teesdale branch for running in locomotives ex-works at Darlington continued during the BR period; in 1957 these included new BR Standard Class 2 2-6-2Ts (the 84XXX series, the last ten of which were built at Darlington). In ordinary service the A8s and G5s predominated, though

Standard 2-6-2T No.84028, having taken water, propels its train out of the siding at Middleton-in-Teesdale; it will then reverse back into the platform ready for its return journey to Darlington. PHOTOGRAPH: J.W.ARMSTRONG TRUST

Middleton-in-Teesdale branch passenger services at selected dates

Through trains:
BISH - Bishop Auckland; DARL - Darlington; DURH - Durham; LEAM - Leamside; NEWC - Newcastle-upon-Tyne; SUND - Sunderland

Times:
dot (as in 7.13) denotes a.m; slash (as in 1/13) denotes p.m.

Notes:
M - mixed train; NS - ran non-stop between Barnard Castle and Middleton-in-Teesdale; SO - Saturdays only; SX - Saturdays excepted THuO - Tuesdays and Thursdays only; TThX - Tuesdays and Thursdays excepted; WO - Wednesdays only; WSO - Wednesdays and Saturdays only

TVR - May 1868 (first timetable)

	Weekdays only		
Middleton	7.25	11.35	5/00
B.Castle	7.47	11.57	5/22
B.Castle	· 8.05	1/40	7/45
Middleton	8.28	2/03	8/08

TVR - February 1870

	Weekdays only			
Notes		WO (M)		
Middleton	7.25	9.15	11.35	5/00
B.Castle	7.47	9.45	11.57	5/22
B.Castle	8.05	1/40	7/45	
Middleton	8.28	2/03	8/08	

TVR - July 1873

	Weekdays only					
Middleton	6.25	8.55	12.00	2/20	4/50	8/00
B.Castle	6.45	9.15	12/20	2/40	5/10	8/20
B.Castle	8.05	11.20	1/43	4/10	7/22	8/55
Middleton	8.27	11.42	2/05	4/32	7/44	9/17

NER - August 1902

	Weekdays only						
Middleton	6.45	8.15	12/02	2/22	5/40	8/15	
B.Castle	7.07	8.37	12/24	2/44	6/02	8/37	
B.Castle	7.42	11.13	1/33	4/43	6/25	9/16	9/40
Middleton	8.05	11.36	1/56	5/06	6/48	9/39	10/03
						TThO	TThX

NER - July 1921

	Weekdays						Sundays
			WO				
Middleton	6.46	8.16	9.36	2/10	5/35		5/35
B.Castle	7.06	8.36	9.58	2/30	6/01		5/59
To	BISH	DURH		BISH	DURH		DARL
From	LEAM						DARL
B.Castle	7.41	9.00	1/36	4/49	6/30		9.35
Middleton	8.05	9.22	1/58	5/11	6/52		9.58
		WO					

in certain circumstances - particularly on Bank Holidays - one might see Standard Class 3 and 4 2-6-0s or ex-LNER J39 0-6-0s.

During 1957 many of the local services in the North-east were given over to diesel multiple-units. The Middleton-in-Teesdale branch was not immune from the DMU incursion, but they did not take over completely until the commencement of that year's winter timetable on 16 September. The DMUs were Metro-Cammell sets, and as these were based at Darlington (where there was a new diesel depot) the engine shed at Middleton-in-Teesdale became redundant and was closed, though it was not demolished until the summer of 1961.

The last occupant of the shed (in 1957) was G5 No.67305. The branch goods workings which, by this time, dealt almost exclusively with stone traffic from the quarries near Middleton-in-Teesdale, remained steam hauled.

The DMU services on the Middleton-in-Teesdale branch settled down to a basic pattern of five each way on weekdays. There was, however, an additional working from Darlington to Middleton early on Monday mornings so that the diesel set was in position for the first train of the day from Middleton, and also an additional Saturday evening working from Middleton to Darlington which enabled the diesel set to return to its home depot for the week-end. Teesdale continued to be a popular location for excursions, and special trains were laid on at certain times. One such excursion ran from Sunderland on Whit Monday (3 June) 1963, hauled by 'Type 2' diesel (Class 24) D5149.

The branch's regular DMU services continued only until 1964. The last day of scheduled passenger services was Saturday 28 November, the usual two-car set being made up to four cars in anticipation of 'last day' crowds. The branch remained open to goods traffic for another four months or so, and closed completely as from Monday 5 April 1965. The branch's more celebrated neighbour, the Stainmore line across the Pennines to Kirkby Stephen, had closed to traffic in January 1962 and lifting had commenced soon after, but the section between Barnard Castle and Tees Valley Junction had been retained as it was, of course, used by Middleton branch trains.

Despite having been abandoned well over thirty years ago, the route of the Middleton-in-Teesdale branch can be clearly traced in many places although there is limited scope for a lengthy, unbroken 'trackbed' walk. Three of the four branch stations still stand: the platform buildings at Cotherstone and Romaldkirk are now private houses, while the station yard at Middleton-in-Teesdale is now occupied by the Daleview Country Club and Caravan Park, with the station buildings as their offices.

Contributors' note: *During the preparation of this article, considerable reference was made to Tees Valley Railway and North Eastern Railway minute books, Board of Trade documents and public and working timetables, all of which were sourced at the Public Record Office at Kew. Secondary sources include* The North Eastern Railway *by William Weaver Tomlinson,* Memories of the LNER in South-west Durham *by A.W.Stobbs (1969),* The Stainmore Railway *by Ken Hoole (Dalesman, 1973),* North Eastern Locomotive Sheds, *also by Ken Hoole (David & Charles, 1972),* Dam Builders Railways *by Harold Bowtell, and the famous 'Green Guide' - formally known as* Locomotives of the LNER - *published by the RCTS.*

LNER - March 1940

	Weekdays only								
								SX	
Middleton	6.50	8.12	10.30	11.50	2/30	3/45	5/20	6/40	8/10
B.Castle	7.12	8.32	10.50	12/10	2/54	4/05	5/40	7/02	8/30
To	DARL	DURH	DARL	DURH		DARL	BISH		BISH
From	DURH	DARL	DURH	DARL		BISH	DARL		
B.Castle	7.34	9.42	11.21	1/57	3/05	4/46	5/54	7/21	9/30
Middleton	7.58	10.06	11.38	2/19	3/30	5/08	6/17	7/46	9/54
			NS				SX		

LNER - November 1946

	Weekdays								
									SO
Middleton	6.40	7.50	10.12	11.45	2/10	3/48	5/43	6/55	9/15
B.Castle	7.02	8.10	10.32	12/07	2/32	4/08	6/03	7/15	9/35
To	DARL	DARL	DURH	SUND	DARL	DARL	SUND	DARL	
From	DARL	SUND	DURH ?	SUND	DARL	SUND	DARL	DARL	
B.Castle	6.58	9.32	10.46	12/30	2/55	4/57	6/18	7/50	10/00
Middleton	7.20	9.54	11.08	12/52	3/17	5/19	6/40	8/12	10/22
									SO

	Sundays	
8.00	6/50	9/00
8.20	7/10	9/20
	DARL	DARL
	DARL	DARL
9.35	5/50	8/28
9.57	6/13	8/50

LNER - October 1947

	Weekdays					
Middleton	6.40	7.50	11.40	3/35	5/40	6/55
B.Castle	7.01	8.10	12/02	3/55	6/01	7/16
To	DARL	SUND	SUND	DARL	SUND	DARL
From	NEWC	SUND	DARL	SUND	DARL	DARL
B.Castle	7.13	10.47	1/13	5/01	6/18	7/50
Middleton	7.35	11.09	1/25	5/23	6/41	8/14

	Sundays	
8.00	6/50	9/00
8.20	7.10	9/20
-	DARL	DARL
DARL	DARL	DARL
9.35	5/53	8/28
9.57	6/16	8/50

BR - July 1957

	Weekdays only						
	SX	SO					
Middleton	7.55	10.12	10.38	11.40	2/14	5/53	6/40
B.Castle	8.17	10.32	10.58	12/04	2/34	6/16	7/02
To	SUND	DARL	DARL	BISH *	DARL	SUND	DARL
From	DARL ?	DARL	SUND	DARL	SUND?	DARL ?	DARL ?
B.Castle	7.02	8.53	11.02	1/25	5/18	6/12	9/44
Middleton	7.24	9.15	11.24	1/47	5/40	6/34	10/06

* On Mondays-Fridays, train continues to Durham

After the closure of the Middleton-in-Teesdale branch, Romaldkirk station was converted to a private house. The signal was, however, not part of the original railway furniture. This picture was taken on 29 July 1986. PHOTOGRAPH: IAN S.CARR

TOM ON TOUR
Photographs by Tom Heavyside

As regular readers of *Railway Bylines* magazine will know, we often feature photographs by Tom Heavyside. From the 1960s onwards, young Mr.Heavyside, like many of his contemporaries, cannily realised that although steam was rapidly disappearing from the BR network, there was still a fair bit of steam activity in the industrial sector in Britain. Consequently, during the next couple of decades Mr.H travelled the length and breadth of the land to record industrial steam before it, too, disappeared. He had - and still has - a marvellous eye for a picture, as evidenced by this quartet, positively oozing with workmanlike character and grit.

For our photo features, we usually try to find a common factor to link the photographs; here, though, we're winging it a little, as the best link we can offer is that the four pictures were all taken in the 1970s. That embarrassingly tenuous connection takes us to Bersham Colliery at Wrexham (top left) on 21 August 1973 with Hawthorn Leslie 0-4-0ST W/No.3072 SHAKESPEARE and spoil tip in background, and to the NCB's engine shed at Niddrie, near Edinburgh, (lower left) on 8 May 1972 with the landsale yard shunter, Andrew Barclay 0-6-0ST W/No.2358. On 28 August 1974 young Mr.Heavyside was at Vane Tempest Colliery at Seaham (top right), photographing Bagnall 'Austerity' 0-6-0ST W/No.2775, while a few months earlier, on 23 May 1974, he had been at Polkemmet Colliery in West Lothian (lower right) where Andrew Barclay 0-6-0ST W/No.1175 was in steam. Sights such as these almost made one forget that BR steam had finished years before.

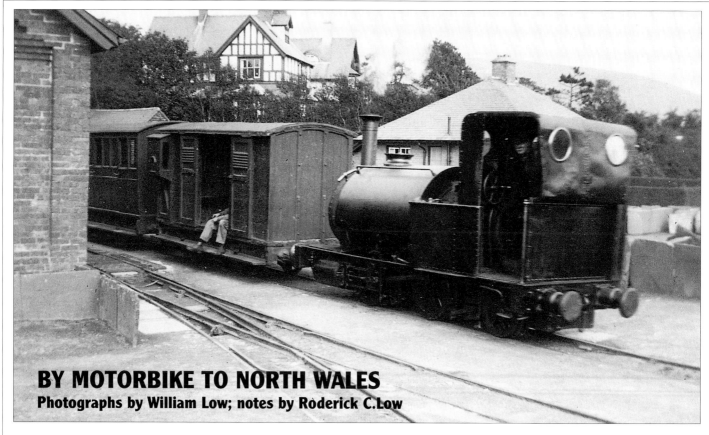

BY MOTORBIKE TO NORTH WALES
Photographs by William Low; notes by Roderick C.Low

On the day of Mr.Low's visit to the Talyllyn Railway, 0-4-2ST TALYLLYN was in action. The locomotive had been built by Fletcher Jennings of Whitehaven, a firm which had started life in 1830 as Messrs.Tulk & Ley and continued in locomotive construction until 1912, latterly trading as the New Lowca Engineering Co. TALYLLYN was built in 1864 (it was ex-works on 24 September of that year, carrying Works No.42) as an 0-4-0ST with 8" x 16" outside cylinders and 2' 4" diameter driving wheels, but was rebuilt in January 1867 as an 0-4-2ST. The Talyllyn Railway purchased an 0-4-0 well tank from the same maker in 1865 - this was W/No.63, which was named DOLGOCH. Although the Talyllyn had been built primarily to transport slate, it also operated a basic passenger service; by the mid-1930s there were three passenger trains each way on weekdays with additional ones at holiday periods. Mr.Low photographed TALYLLYN at Towyn Wharf while it was manoeuvring passenger stock; the vehicle next to the locomotive is the company's distinctive

brake-luggage-booking van. An ancient cove, presumably the driver, peers from the footplate; could the owner of the pair of legs in the booking van be the fireman? Fortunately, TALYLLYN is still with us today, still operating on traditional territory. A visit to the Talyllyn Railway on 20 July 1938 - three or four years after Mr.Low's motorbike tour - was reported in the *Railway Observer* magazine. It was noted that TALYLLYN - '...the locomotive which is used on the existing services...' - was painted green, lined out in red, white and black, though there was no sign of a name painted on the tanks; it was fitted with a '...pull-out type of regulator and hand brake, for there is no continuous braking on the train'. Our visitor in July 1938 reported that the 9.25am train to Abergynolwyn was composed of two coaches, one brake van and three slate trucks, and departed on time from Towyn Wharf '...with the safety valves blowing off at 65lbs per sq. in.'

My paternal grandfather, Robert Low, became an engine driver in 1902 at St.Margaret's shed in Edinburgh and continued to work there (apart from a short, but much enjoyed, stint at North Berwick) until 1941 when he died, still in harness. On the links which my grandfather worked, 'having your own engine' was unusual, but he actually had No.678 - a 'C' class, later LNER J36, - 0-6-0 for several years and was extremely proud of it.

Given the nature of my grandfather's employment, it was not altogether surprising that his son - my father, who was born in 1907 - developed an interest in railways. As a consequence of innumerable footplate rides and mixing with his father's workmates, he knew a lot, too. Indeed, he wanted to become an engineer - a civil engineer (steel bridges fascinated him!) - but by the time he was leaving school, heavy engineering was already in decline and so he opted for what his father called, not unkindly, a 'soft' job in the insurance business. My father qualified as an actuary and spent the rest of his life working either in insurance or for the government and, I believe, regretted every single minute of it.

My father didn't get married until he was thirty-one, and so he had plenty of time to pursue his hobbies and interests. These included, not only railways, but also photography - a potentially intriguing combination! - and he made at least two photographic trips away from home territory in Edinburgh. One trip took him all over the Scottish Border area and down to the north of Cumberland; it produced, among other things, several photographs of ex-NB Atlantics at Steele Road and LM Compounds pounding out of Carlisle but, unfortunately, the pictures weren't of particularly good quality.

The other trip was a solo foray to North Wales. For transport he used a 'James' motorcycle - yes, all the way from Edinburgh! - which he bought in about 1930. 'James' was a Birmingham bicycle maker who had started with motorcycles in a small way in 1902; full-scale production had commenced in the 1920s with a range of 250cc to 750cc machines, some single cylinder, others Vee-twin. I think my father's bike was towards the less ferocious end of the scale. He rode the bike until about 1937 when he went into a wall - the wall came first, my father and his bike

came joint second, and after this incident he seemed to lose his nerve for two-wheeled transport. He didn't switch to four wheels - he never learned to drive a car - and so after the 'wall versus father' affair it was down to public transport. As for the 'James' motorcycle firm, they were taken over by AMC (of Francis-Barnett fame) in 1951 and the whole lot went out of business in 1966.

My father's trip to North Wales and the Welsh Marches is shrouded in mystery. It was certainly viewed as an opportunity to explore the railways in a part of Britain he had never visited before. He took many pictures on the main lines - LNWR 4-6-0s, GWR Dean Goods, a small GWR 2-4-0T, and 'outside swingers' (as he used to call double-framed engines). The picture of GWR No.680, which became something of a celebrity in the April/May 1998 issue of *Railway Bylines* magazine, was also taken on this trip. There is also a picture of the locomotive CARLISLE on the Bishops Castle Railway (my father inexplicably referred to this as 'Merrie Carlisle'), several on the Shropshire & Montgomeryshire, and a number of non-railway subjects such as the canal aque-

A closer view of the Talyllyn's brake-luggage-booking van - note the booking guichet. The picture seems to be taken 'up the top' at Abergynolwyn.

duct at Chirk and the River Severn at Shrewsbury. Frustratingly, I can't recall the exact year of the trip, but it was summertime and, while *en route*, he took a photograph of a brand-new LMS Jubilee at Chester - no nameplates fitted - so it must have been either 1934 or 1935.

While 'on tour', my father stayed in Bed & Breakfasts. He liked to tell a story about one particularly mean-spirited landlady who had an overflow cut in the bath about three inches from the bottom - this meant that her guests could not use much hot water. But she clearly reckoned without a rebellious improviser, as my father simply stuffed a flannel over the hole and held it there with his foot while he enjoyed a good soaking! My father certainly loved the North Wales quarries. Perhaps the sad beauty of the places caught his imagination as much as they did mine in later dec-

Llechwedd State Quarries, to the north of Blaenau Ffestiniog, were opened up by J.W.Greaves & Sons *circa* 1846. In 1848 the quarries were connected to the Festiniog Railway by means of a lengthy incline - this is clearly evident in the photograph. The sharply inclined bridge crossing the foot of the incline carries the A470 road which leads to Betws-y-Coed (left) and the centre of Blaenau Ffestiniog (right); the bridge is known as 'The Crimea'. The second arch, just to the right of the one over the incline, crosses a small river. The power station, which provided the electricity for various quarry operations, is clearly identified sandwiched between the road and river. In the foreground we can see Oakeley Wharf where some of the slate from the Oakeley Quarries (behind the photographer, well out of view) was loaded direct on to standard gauge wagons on the L&NWR's Llandudno Junction-Blaenau Ffestiniog branch. The L&NWR branch - the running line can be seen behind the wagons - passes through a tunnel to the north of Blaenau Ffestiniog; the south portal of the tunnel is only just out of view on the left. In 1972 part of the quarry was taken over for use as a tourist centre, Lechwedd Slate Caverns.

One of the most distinctive, albeit not particularly beautiful, locomotives working on the Oakeley Quarries 2ft gauge system was a 28hp four-wheel petrol-mechanical machine, built by the German firm of Gasmoteren Fabrik Deutz *circa* 1920. It was purchased second-hand by the quarry company in 1929 and remained on site until being scrapped in 1964, though it had been out of use since the early 1950s, if not before. This picture is thought to have been taken near the viaduct which carried the narrow gauge quarry railway over the L&NWR branch on the northern outskirts of Blaenau Ffestiniog.

ades. Although, at the time of his visit, the quarrying industry was bigger and more prosperous than during my visits of the 1960s, there would still have been that air of dignified decay, and everywhere the vast grey rain-sodden rock. For every active quarry, there were ten like those we can visit today - trackless inclines, roofless buildings, rusting machinery, broken rock - the mute reminders of past human endeavour.

I imagine that the absence of further trips and more photographs can be put down to my father's lack of money and transport at that time - he was studying for about ten years while articled to the 'Century Life' offices in Edinburgh. Nevertheless, from the mid-1930s he regularly purchased the *Railway Magazine* and kept his father's meagre collection of technical railway books. When I came along - 'added to stock' is a term which springs to mind - my father had an excuse to indulge his old interests occasionally; the family had, by then, moved to London, and I was brought up to stand patiently at the end of 'No.10' at Kings Cross. Long journeys to Edinburgh to visit relatives were invariably punctuated by his "...Grantham shed's on the left in a minute" or "...we're approaching Newcastle - look out for North Eastern 0-8-0s".

Returning to the matter of my father's trip to North Wales in the 1930s, he passed the photographs on to me - as, indeed, he did with all his other photographs - but I must concede that few have yielded satisfactory enlargements (despite the efforts of a first-rate printer!). This little selection is the best of the bunch. (*We regret that copies of these photographs are not available* - Ed).

Oakeley Slate Quarries were a little to the north-west of Blaenau Ffestiniog on the opposite side of the L&NWR line to Llechwedd Quarries. There were three main quarries - two were opened up by Samuel Holland, the first in 1819 and the second in 1826, while the third was opened by Messrs.Matthews & Huddart in 1833. In the 1880s, all three were taken over by the newly formed Oakeley Slate Quarries Company. Oakeley's were a forward-looking company, and installed electrically operated machinery for pumping and slate preparation as early as 1906.

Each of the three quarries had its own incline down to the Festiniog Railway; there was also a direct rail connection, by means of the Oakeley's 2ft-gauge railway, into the yard of the L&NWR terminus at Blaenau Ffestiniog. On his visit in the 1930s Mr.Low took this superb photograph looking head-on up one of the three quarry inclines. A rake of loaded slate wagons - of typical North Wales 'slate tram' design - stand on the right while a solitary empty wagon holds the cable at the foot of the incline. Note the telegraph poles clambering away alongside the incline. Slate is still extracted here, albeit on a much reduced scale and without any railway operations; the quarrying operations have been conducted in conjunction with the Gloddfa Ganol tourist centre, which recently had a collection of locomotives and rolling stock on display at the site.

Today, the Festiniog Railway is, arguably, the best known of all the North Wales narrow gauge railways; that is largely due to the efforts of the preservationists who took over the disused railway in 1954 and, with commendable perseverance and energy, began the long task of turning it into what it is today. As a slate carrying railway, the Festiniog Railway, at its peak, conveyed up to 150,000 tons of slate and some 150,000 passengers annually, but by the 1930s, when Mr.Low made his photographic visit, things were in serious decline. Indeed, a visitor to the line a few years later – in May 1938 – reported that there were just two slate trains each day, hauled by a petrol locomotive.

The northern extremity of the Festiniog Railway was at Duffws, a couple of hundred yards beyond the station which it shared with the GWR. Mr.Low photographed PRINCE, one of the Festiniog's celebrated George England 0-4-0STs, on shunting duties at Duffws – it seems that this was an unusual opportunity as PRINCE apparently worked very rarely during the 1930s. It was reported in July 1938 that only three steam locomotives were in

service – 0-4-0ST No.1 PRINCESS, and two Fairlie 0-4-4-0Ts, No.3 TALIEISIN and No.10 MERDDIN EMRYS – along with a 1917-built Simplex petrol locomotive. The passenger service, which by this time operated only during the summer, comprised two trains each way: 10.20am and 3.10pm from Portmadoc and 12.05pm and 4.20pm from Blaenau Ffestiniog.

Returning to Mr.Low's photograph, the building on the left is the old goods shed, the rails having been lifted and the gaps in the granite setts having been filled in with what appears to be tarmac; the goods shed was demolished in the 1950s and the space used as a car park. The structure partly visible on the extreme right-hand edge of the picture is the rear of the already disused platform building – Duffws station had closed to passenger traffic in 1931 – though the building still stands and, when visited in 1961 was used, somewhat ignominiously, as a public convenience. As for PRINCE, this was one of the Festiniog locomotives which was saved for preservation. It is now 134 years old.

FOURUM -THROUGH THE STREETS
Photographs by Bob Griffiths

Of all the 'street' railways in Britain, one of the best known is undoubtedly the Weymouth Harbour Tramway where locomotives hauled the Channel Islands boat trains - usually lengthy ensembles of corridor stock - or substantial goods trains through the streets to and from the harbour. As sure as night followed day, the passage of a train through the streets would be halted somewhere along the way by a thoughtlessly parked car. And it wasn't as if there weren't any warning notices or road markings... However, there were usually plenty of pedestrians walking through the streets, and so there was enough man-power on hand to 'bounce' an offending car out of the way. To holidaymakers unaccustomed to this local eccentricity, the procedure of man-handling cars out of the way no doubt prompted a comment or two when the postcards were being written, but the railway staff who had to cope with it all, day in and day out, viewed things with rather less amusement. Between 1935 and 1962, duties on the Weymouth Harbour Tramway were usually entrusted to the GWR's 1366 class 0-6-0PTs - the distinctive short-wheelbase outside-cylinder 'matchboxes'. All five of the class, Nos.1366-1371, had spells at Weymouth at various times, three usually being there simultaneously.

This sequence of pictures shows No.1368's progress one day in the late summer of 1959. In the top left photograph, the locomotive - running bunker-first towards the harbour, as was the usual practice - passes Westham Road Crossing. The bowling greens are visible on the far left. The train includes oil tank wagons (with bunkering fuel), vans (presumably to be loaded with perishable farm produce or flowers from the Channel Islands) and conflats. Note the locomotive's bell. In the lower left picture, No.1368's driver keeps a watch on clearances as the train is hauled around Ferry's Corner towards the Town Bridge. The top right picture shows the train after it has passed under the Town Bridge and continues along Custom House Quay - at the point where the tramway passes around the corner in the distance, the line becomes double track. Finally, in the lower right picture, No.1368 has deposited its train at the quay and is running round, either in readiness to head back to Weymouth Junction with another train or to look after a spot of shunting at the harbour. The ship, the M.V.ST.HELIER, is one of a pair which had been built for the GWR in 1925; the sister ship was the M.V.ST.JULIEN. Wish you were here...

In Terrier Territory
EMLEY MOOR AND PARK MILL COLLIERIES
by Adrian Booth

When considering the Yorkshire coalfield, the West Riding town of Huddersfield and its environs do not immediately spring to mind. This is despite the fact that, only about ten miles or so to the east one finds Barnsley and Wakefield, which once had an enormously productive coalfield. However, Huddersfield *does* have other claims to fame, such as its textile industry. Some might also regard Huddersfield Town Football Club as a local claim to fame *(really??? - Ed)*, though some of its supporters have, arguably, achieved greater prominence than the club itself - among the 'past and present' supporters of 'The Terriers' are the late Prime Minister Harold Wilson and, more recently, Patrick Stewart, the actor who plays Captain Jean-Luc Picard in the cult TV series *Star Trek*. Indeed, Mirfield-born Patrick Stewart has boldly gone where no other Star Trek actor has gone before, having supported Huddersfield Town for over forty-five years.

Nevertheless, Huddersfield was not completely excluded from the mining map

Above. Over the years, four different Hudswell Clarke 0-4-0STs were employed by Emley Moor Colliery for use at the screens near Skelmanthorpe station. One of the four was STANDBACK No.2, which was delivered new in April 1905 and spent all its life there, until being unceremoniously scrapped in 1979. This picture was taken on 31 August 1967. PHOTOGRAPH: ROGER MONK

Right. A little to the east of Emley Moor Colliery was Park Mill Colliery, the screens of which were adjacent to Clayton West station. When visited on 21 January 1978 a number of 16-ton mineral wagons were waiting to be loaded at the screens. PHOTOGRAPH: ADRIAN BOOTH

As explained in the text, the screens which dealt with the coal from Emley Moor Colliery were near Skelmanthorpe station. This view of the screens was taken on 22 May 1979. The engine shed is seen on the extreme left while, above it in the far distance, is the famous Emley Moor television mast. The locomotive is Thomas Hill W/No.158c. PHOTOGRAPH: ADRIAN BOOTH

of England. There are records of coal mining in the Huddersfield district (at Emley) as far back as 1357 and, in later centuries, as demand for household coal increased, numerous shallow pits were scattered over the area. The thin Pot Clay seam was well known, together with its usually attendant fireclay, and hence a pottery industry developed; at one time there was also an

iron industry in the area, albeit on a relatively small scale. By the beginning of the eighteenth century all the principal landowners were issuing coal leases, although the main sinkings - in the Emley and Flockton area to the east of Huddersfield - were less than 300 feet deep. Speedwell Colliery at Emley Moor worked coal from the New Hards seam. These pre-industrial

revolution days were, unfortunately, not without human suffering. It was commonplace in the area to employ children (called hurriers), who crawled along underground tunnels carrying coal in wicker baskets strapped to their backs. The contents were then tipped into large tubs which in turn were pushed and tugged along by women to the bottom of the shaft, where a gin was

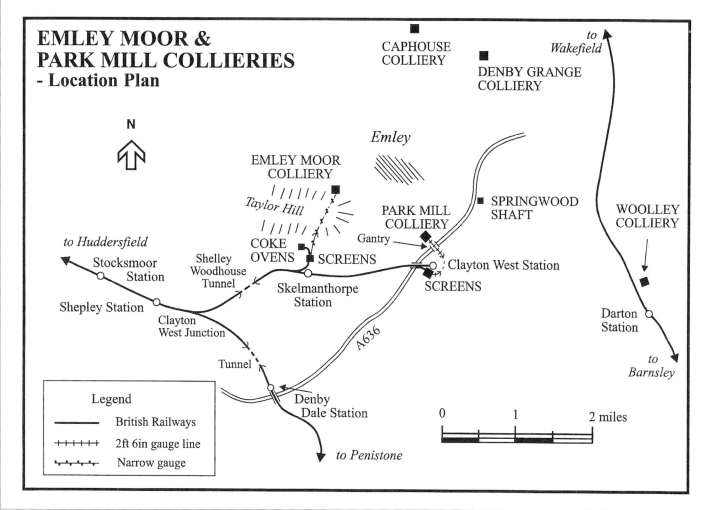

EMLEY MOOR & PARK MILL COLLIERIES
- Location Plan

N

CAPHOUSE COLLIERY

DENBY GRANGE COLLIERY

to Wakefield

Emley

EMLEY MOOR COLLIERY

Taylor Hill

PARK MILL COLLIERY

SPRINGWOOD SHAFT

WOOLLEY COLLIERY

Gantry

COKE OVENS

SCREENS

Clayton West Station

SCREENS

to Huddersfield

Stocksmoor Station

Shelley Woodhouse Tunnel

Skelmanthorpe Station

A636

Darton Station

Shepley Station

Clayton West Junction

to Barnsley

Tunnel

Denby Dale Station

to Penistone

Legend

————	British Railways
+++++	2ft 6in gauge line
·+·+·+·	Narrow gauge

0   1   2 miles

The main Park Mill Colliery buildings and headgears were on the north side of the A636 road. A 2ft 6in gauge track ran across a gantry above the road to reach this tippler house, alongside the headgear. The view was recorded on 21 January 1978. Note the dual gauge track, a legacy of an earlier narrow gauge system employed when the original drift was in use. PHOTOGRAPH: ADRIAN BOOTH

utilised to draw the coal to the surface. The employment of young children was rife, with five- to eight-year-olds working underground. Fortunately, though, Acts of Parliament were eventually passed, notably the one of August 1842 which prohibited women and young children from working underground. However, that was not good news for Britain's equine population

as, in the larger mines, the women and children were replaced by horses.

The great industrial expansion in the nineteenth century coincided with the maximum development of the coal industry in the Huddersfield area, with pits being established in the Elland, Emley Moor, Holmfirth and Lockwood districts. Demand for coal was high, particularly from

Huddersfield's steam-powered textile mills, and the area's coal was comparatively easily won as all the profitable seams were generally shallow in depth. Their gentle and relatively even inclination meant that they were easy to mine, but the wholesale extraction of the seams - particularly in such shallow mines - led to surface subsidence. It was the normal practice to work

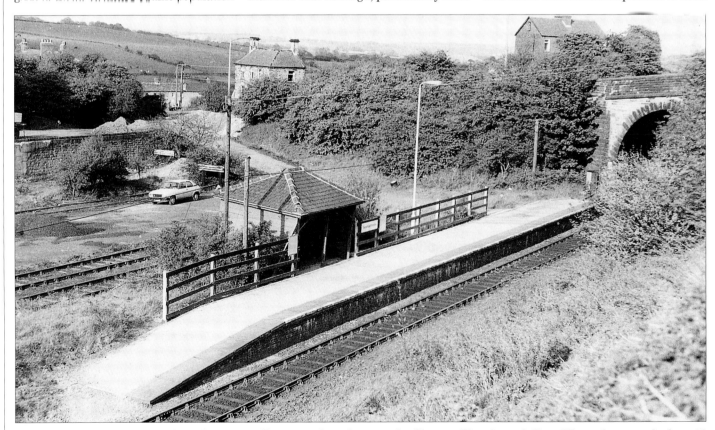

Skelmanthorpe station was the only intermediate stopping place on the Clayton West branch line. When photographed on 16 May 1981, less than two years before the closure of the branch, the station was in rather good nick, with a modern shelter and tidy railings. There had once been a set of steps leading down to the platform from the bridge, but by this time the few remaining passengers had to walk along the path to and from the road. The sidings behind the platform are part of the station goods yard - the colliery screens are out of view to the left. PHOTOGRAPH: ADRIAN BOOTH

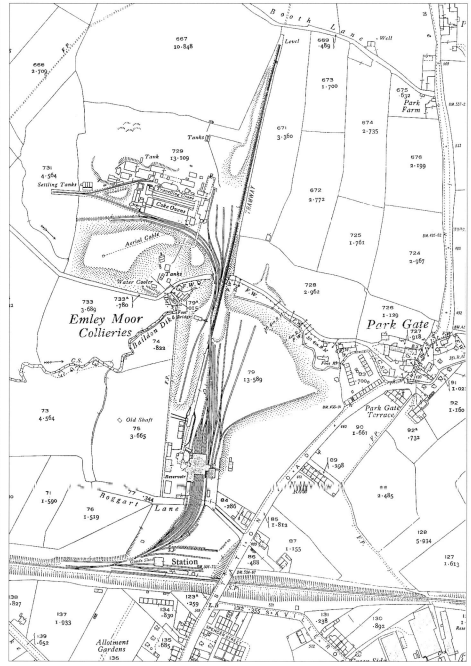

reopened, with the shaft having been widened and deepened. Meanwhile, the Stringer family had become increasingly involved in the local coal industry, having initially prospected for coal at Emley Park Colliery (not to be confused with Emley *Moor* Colliery) at Clayton West. By 1861 Edward Stringer was working the mine (grid reference SE258117), which had by then been renamed Park Mill Colliery. The River Dear passed through the middle of the site.

Railway connections
The standard gauge Huddersfield-Penistone main line (promoted as the Huddersfield & Sheffield Junction Railway, but later part of the Lancashire & Yorkshire Railway) opened on 1 July 1850. It had been an enormous engineering undertaking, as almost the whole course of the line was cutting, embankment, tunnel or viaduct. There were several subsequent proposals - tempted by the prospect of coal and wool traffic - for a branch line to run from the new railway, and through the village of Clayton West to the Dearne Valley. A branch line was eventually authorised on 11 June 1866, but only a line 3½ miles in length terminating at Clayton West. It was not until 27 November 1872 that the first sod was actually cut. The branch was built by the L&Y itself; it was a single-track line which diverged from the main line just to the east of Shepley (at a point which became known, rather logically, as Clayton West Junction) and ran via Skelmanthorpe to Clayton West. The construction of the branch was fraught with problems, especially the boring of the 511-yard long Shelley Woodhouse tunnel, and the line did not open to passenger traffic until 1 September 1879. An intermediate station at Skelmanthorpe was opened on 1 December 1879. The L&Y's intention was that the branch should be extended a few miles farther east to join the Barnsley-Wakefield line at Darton, but although the necessary land was purchased for the extension, and renewed powers were obtained in 1893, the extension was never constructed.

Emley Moor Colliery
Prior to the opening of the Clayton West branch coal from Emley Moor Colliery had been carted away by road, but the arrival of the railway prompted the development of facilities adjacent to Skelmanthorpe station, approximately one mile to the south of the colliery. The facilities included screens which were served by six standard gauge tracks, and coke ovens at the north end of the site. Coal was brought underground from the colliery to Skelmanthorpe Screens in tubs by means of a rope-worked narrow gauge line which ran beneath Taylor Hill. (The alternative of a surface railway line between the colliery and screens was not an option, due to the height of Taylor Hill). The miners went down the shaft at the main Emley Moor Colliery site, and hewed the coal by old-fashioned pillar and stall hand-cutting methods, loading it into the tubs for underground transportation to Skelmanthorpe Screens. The coal emerged on to the surface at Skelmanthorpe, at the north end of the

The wording on this Ordnance Survey map of 1931 is a little confusing, as Emley Moor Colliery was about a mile to the north. What we see here is the set-up at Skelmanthorpe, with the screens immediately to the north of the station on the Clayton West branch, and the coke ovens clearly marked. The tramway running southwards from Booth Lane is the rope-worked narrow gauge underground railway which brought the coal from the colliery itself down to the screens. Note the single platform station, with its modest goods yard, on the Clayton West branch. Please note that, for reasons of space, the map has been reduced from its original scale of 25" to the mile. CROWN COPYRIGHT

'pillar and stall', whereby rectangular pillars of coal were left in place to support the roof. Later opencast excavation revealed some old mines where upwards of thirty per cent of coal had been left in. By 1861 there were no less than forty small coal mines in the area. Production peaked at 384,700 tons in 1867, but by 1872 the figure had dropped to 74,757 tons - there had, in fact, been a significant increase in the demand for coal, but this was more economically met by the numerous deep pits which had been sunk farther east to exploit the rich, thick coal such as in the Barnsley and Silkstone seams.

As already mentioned, coal had been worked from an early date in the Emley Moor area; a little to the east of there, Clayton West was the site of other early workings. As for the latter site, an early reference exists in the form of a lease dated 25 March 1659, which allowed coal mining at Bilham Grange adit mine. Mining at

Bilham Grange took a back seat at harvest time, as the four mine workers had to assist - at their normal mining wage rate - to help bring in the harvest. Other small mines in the vicinity are recorded at Clayton Common, Duke Wood, Hollinhouse, Low Commonside and Toppit - the last-named, which was owned by one James Taylor, was operational until World War I. But for the purpose of this article, we shall look at Emley Moor and Park Mill collieries, the first of which can be traced back to the 1820s.

The 1822 edition of *White's Directory* lists four coal mines then at work in Emley - one was owned by John Bedford, and the other three by the Jagger family. Of the Jagger's mines, one (a pit dating from the 1820s at Emley Moor, grid reference SK236129) was an old shaft of shallow depth which was closed and fenced around by 1837, and reported to be overgrown with blackberry bushes. By 1861 the mine had

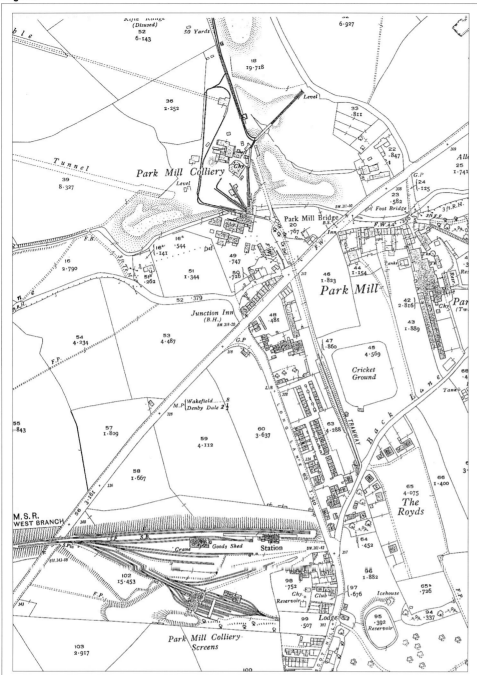

Park Mill Colliery - a reduction from the 25" Ordnance survey map of 1931. The colliery is clearly marked in the upper portion of the map, and the screens are identified adjacent to Clayton West station. The narrow gauge tramway which conveyed the coal from the colliery to the screens can be traced - it leaves the south-eastern corner of the colliery site, is carried over the main road by means of a bridge, then descends an embankment to burrow underground on the north side of Back Lane. It emerges on the surface again in the yard of Clayton West station (next to the 361.42 bench mark) and continues along a gantry (the alignment of which is indicated by the parallel dotted lines) to the screens. A little to the north-east of the colliery we see the original drift mine (indicated as 'level') while In the top left we see the course of the aerial ropeway from Speedwell Colliery. CROWN COPYRIGHT

and Emley Moor Colliery, which was owned by the Jagger family, were amalgamated under the title of Stringer & Jagger Ltd. There followed a period of modernisation. In 1904 the first coal face conveyor was installed at Park Mill Colliery, and in 1909 both collieries were supplied with electricity from the Yorkshire Electric Power Company's generating station at Thornhill; electricity was also supplied to the tied colliery houses. In 1910 an aerial ropeway (part of which seen in the top left of the accompanying map) was erected to convey coal from Speedwell No.2 mine to Park Mill. Before too long, the Jagger family withdrew from coal mining and the collieries passed into sole ownership of Edward Stringer who formed a new company called Stringer & Son Ltd. The early twentieth century witnessed rapid development of coal mining in eastern Yorkshire, and the main coal centres consequently gravitated to that part of the county. The Huddersfield area was left in a relatively minor position, with Stringer's collieries at Emley Moor and Park Mill being the westernmost outpost of the Yorkshire coal industry. The only other mines which remained in the Huddersfield area were small-scale privately owned operations, although seven or eight of these survived until the late 1950s and one, Hay Royds Mine, is still operational today.

On 1 January 1947, all of Britain's collieries were vested in the new National Coal Board (NCB); Emley Moor and Park Mill collieries both came under the administration of the North Barnsley Area. Figures listed in the *Coal Trades Directory* for 1948 show that Emley Moor had an average annual production of 180,000 tons with a staff of 400 underground and 110 surface workers; Park Mill's production was 220,000 tons, with 440 underground and 170 surface employees. The directory stated that both collieries produced coal suitable for gas production, household use, coking and steam.

Locomotives - Skelmanthorpe Screens
The first known shunters at Skelmanthorpe Screens were MOSELEY (Manning Wardle 0-4-0ST W/No.1041 of 1887, which arrived second-hand from Nuttall's, the contractors, probably in the late 1880s, and 0-4-0ST STANDBACK No.1 which was new in March 1897 from Hudswell Clarke of Leeds (W/No.476). The Hudswell Clarke proved itself to be an efficient locomotive and a wise choice for the mine owners, who duly returned to the same builder for an additional engine - this was STANDBACK No.2 (Hudswell Clarke W/No.669), which arrived new in April 1905. The two Hudswell Clarkes and the Manning Wardle soldiered on together for over thirty years.

The Manning Wardle, MOSELEY, was scrapped *circa* September 1937 and was replaced by a diesel locomotive - the use of a diesel was, of course, quite innovative in that era. The locomotive was supplied by John Fowler of Leeds as their W/No.22075 on 10 February 1938 - named IRVING, it was an 80hp 0-4-0 diesel-mechanical. It was to be another twenty years before the motive power roster was supplemented, this time by a second-hand Hudswell

screens, and the tubs were taken down to the screens where the coal was off-loaded and, after grading, transferred in to standard gauge wagons which had been placed under the screens. Some of these coal wagons were shunted round to the coke ovens, while others were despatched via the branch line to customers elsewhere.

Park Mill Colliery
At Park Mill Colliery, coal was brought out of the mine on a narrow gauge railway from an adit just to the north-east of the main buildings. The existence of a coking coal seam led to the construction of six bee-hive coke ovens at Park Mill, and these remained in use until 1920 when the seam was exhausted. The coal from Park Mill Colliery was originally taken to the Clayton West branch terminus by horse and cart, where new screens were erected (at

grid reference SE259112) alongside the station, but by the 1920s the coal was conveyed by a tramway which ran southwards from the colliery. The tramway descended into a tunnel beneath the main road, then emerged on to the surface for a short stretch alongside the village cricket ground, then went underground again near Back Lane, passed below Long Lane, and emerged adjacent to Clayton West station. The tramway tubs were then raised to the level of the screens by means of an enclosed gantry (this is depicted by the double dotted line on the accompanying Ordnance survey map); at the screens, the tubs were tipped and the coal transferred into standard gauge wagons.

Combined forces
To facilitate operations, Park Mill Colliery, which was owned by the Stringer family,

STANDBACK No.1, built by Hudswell Clarke in 1897, was Emley Moor's first new locomotive. It was transferred to Bentley Colliery at Doncaster in 1953 and subsequently found its way to Harworth Colliery, where it was scrapped in 1959. PHOTOGRAPH: FRANK JONES

frame of an old 4-wheel Sentinel steam locomotive. On to the frame was built modern-style diesel bodywork, housing a Rolls-Royce 179hp engine coupled to a hydraulic transmission. This machine was the last arrival at Skelmanthorpe Screens. It bore running number TL39, a legacy of its former home at South Kirkby Colliery (a number of Barnsley Area NCB locomotives had 'TL' prefixes to their numbers), and was painted green with red buffer beams and coupling rods.

Skelmanthorpe's veteran Fowler diesel, IRVING, was disposed of in 1979, being cut up on site by scrap merchants W.Bush & Son of Alfreton on Thursday 17 May 1979. The scrap, including the Fowler 6-cylinder engine, was taken away in two lorries the following Thursday. This left the Thomas Hill diesel to soldier on alone, without any resident cover.

The locomotives employed at Skelmanthorpe Screens were housed in a rather distinctive brick-built shed. The building was, in effect, two dead-end sheds back-to-back - a locomotive could enter at either end, but could not run through from one end to the other; each half had its own inspection pit and could accommodate one engine. Externally, though, the structure looked every bit like a continuous 'single unit', with six windows on each side, wooden doors (latterly painted red) at each end, and a flat roof on which was mounted a diesel fuel tank.

Locomotives - Park Mill

Standard gauge locomotive working at Park Mill screens was not instigated until August 1969. The first resident locomotive was John Fowler 0-4-0 diesel-mechanical W/No.22558, which was of the same

Clarke 0-4-0ST (W/No.614 of 1902) which, prior to its arrival at Skelmanthorpe Screens *circa* 1958, had worked at Haigh Colliery, a few miles to the east near Darton. Ten years on, in February 1968, another second-hand Hudswell Clarke 0-4-0ST (W/No.1817 of 1953) arrived at Skelmanthorpe Screens, this time from Hartley Bank Colliery near Horbury. It was named STANDBACK No.3.

Skelmanthorpe's Hudswell Clarke W/No.614 was scrapped in January 1969, W/No.669 (STANDBACK No.2) *circa* October 1970, and W/No.1817 (STANDBACK No.3) - the last steam locomotive on site - in September 1976. STANDBACK No.3 had latterly been kept as cover for the long-term resident - and now veteran - Fowler diesel but, in practice, the duties at the screens were relatively light and the Fowler managed very well on its own. Nevertheless, as a precautionary measure, the NCB transferred another diesel to the site in October 1975; this was Thomas Hill W/No.158c, which had been built at the maker's Kilnhurst Works in 1965 utilising the

Hudswell Clarke W/No.669 was new to Emley Moor on 26 April 1905; it was named STANDBACK No.2. It was resting beside the engine shed at Skelmanthorpe Screens on 28 June 1969. PHOTOGRAPH: ADRIAN BOOTH

SUMMARY OF LOCOMOTIVES
Makers abbreviated thus: HC - Hudswell Clarke; **JF** - John Fowler; **MW** - Manning Wardle; **TH/S** - Thomas Hill/Sentinel
(a) Emley Moor Colliery - standard gauge locomotives used at Skelmanthorpe Screens

Name/number	Type	Maker W/No.	Built	Wheel diameter	Cyls. (o); h.p.	Date acquired	Disposal	Notes
MOSELEY	0-4-0ST	MW; 1041	1887			c.1880s	Scr. c.9.1937	ex-Nuttall (contractors)
STANDBACK No.1	0-4-0ST	HC; 476	3.1897	2' 9"	10" x 16"	New	Moved 1953	To Bentley Colliery
-	0-4-0ST	HC; 614	6.1902	3' 1"	13" x 18"	c.1958	Scr. 1.1969	ex-Haigh Colliery
STANDBACK No.2	0-4-0ST	HC; 669	4.1905	3' 1"	12" x 18"	New	Scr. c.10.1979	
STANDBACK No.3	0-4-0ST	HC; 1817	5.1953	3' 3½"	14" x 22"	2.1968	Scr. 9.1976	ex-Hartley Bank Colliery
IRVING	0-4-0DM	JF; 22075	2.1938		80hp	New	Scr. 5.1979	
TL39	4w DH	TH/S; 158c	10.1965	2' 6"	179hp	10.1975	Sold 2.1984	Later resold - see text

(b) Park Mill Colliery - standard gauge surface locomotives used at the screens

Name/number	Type	Maker W/No.	Built	Wheel diameter	H.p.	Date acquired	Disposal	Notes
-	0-4-0DM	JF; 22558	5.1939		80hp	8.1969	Scr. c.4.1976	
-	0-4-0DM	HC; D1094	8.1959	2' 6½"	72hp	10.1972	Moved c.7.1981	To Gascoine Wood Colliery

(c) Park Mill Colliery - 2' 6" gauge underground flameproof locomotives

Name	Type	Maker W/No.	Built	Wheel diameter	H.p.	Date acquired	Disposal	Notes
ALICIA	0-4-0DM	HC; DM746	8.1951	2' 0"	68hp	New	Moved 8.1990	To Yorkshire Mining Museum
HELEN	0-4-0DM	HC; DM747	8.1951	2' 0"	68hp	New	Moved 12.1985	To Prince of Wales Colliery
ROSEMARY	0-4-0DM	HC; DM748	10.1951	2' 0"	68hp	New	Moved 8.1990	To Yorkshire Mining Museum
VERONICA	0-4-0DM	HC; DM890	2.1955	2' 0"	68hp	New	Moved 12.1985	To Prince of Wales Colliery
DEBORAH	0-4-0DM	HC; DM1356	3.1965	2' 0"	68hp	New	Moved 8.1990	To Yorkshire Mining Museum
-	0-4-0DM	HC; DM704	1948	2' 0"	68hp	10.1976	Scr. c.1977	

design and vintage as Skelmanthorpe's long term resident diesel. The Park Mill diesel had been built in May 1939 for Powell Duffryn of Caerphilly, but had later moved to Barnsley Main Colliery and then, *circa* September 1967, to Dearne Valley Colliery, near Barnsley. On arriving at Park Mill, it was put to work shunting the small screens and forming wagons into rakes to be taken away by BR along the branch line.

The standard gauge locomotives at Park Mill were never treated to the luxury of a shed; the locomotives simply stood under cover beneath the screens. In October 1972 a second locomotive was brought to Park Mill Colliery to help out their old Fowler diesel. The new arrival was Hudswell Clarke W/No.D1094, a small 72hp 0-4-0 diesel-mechanical which the NCB had purchased new in August 1959 to shunt light traffic at their Barnsley Area central workshops at Shafton. When it had become redundant there it had moved, in January 1971, to Grimethorpe Colliery, before finally moving to Park Mill. The Fowler diesel at Park Mill was finally laid aside in the mid-1970s and was scrapped on site by Thos.W.Ward Ltd *circa* April 1976.

Underground locomotives
The NCB invested heavily in Britain's coal mines, and Park Mill saw the benefit in 1951 when its underground workings were dieselised. By this time the undergound railway had been provided with a new 'drift' (this was the 'passageway' which took the railway underground) on the south side of the A636 road, while a spindly steel bridge - which looked like a primitive gantry, it must be said! - took the railway above the road and across to the main colliery complex. Initially, three 2ft 6in gauge flameproof diesel-mechanical locomotives were purchased from Hudswell Clarke of Leeds (W/Nos. DM746-748); a fourth, similar, machine, W/No.DM890, arrived in 1955,

and a fifth, also similar, W/No.DM1356, in 1965. When delivered, the flameproof locomotives were painted green and lined out in red; all five were later named (see table), the names being chosen by the shed foreman, Mr.Cooke, who opted for the names of his wife, children, and other family members. The names were painted on, but in the early 1970s they were obliterated when the locomotives were repainted white; in place of names, the locomotives received running numbers which corresponded with their works numbers (for example, W/No.890 became fleet No.890). In October 1976 the underground locomotive fleet was supplemented by Hudswell Clarke W/No.DM704, transferred from Grimethorpe Colliery at Barnsley, but it did not perform any work at Park Mill as it was cannibalised by the fitters for any useful spares - its wheelsets and Gardner engine were put in the stores, and the rest was scrapped.

The fleet usually remained underground during the working week, with three locomotives working on coal traffic and one on man-riding 'Paddy' duties. By May 1979 the coal workings were some four miles from the point where the railway went undergound. The locomotives were provided with a single track shed at the top of the 1 in 12 'drift'; the shed was capable of accommodating three locomotives, and at any one time there was usually one locomotive undergoing repair or a major service there. Three or four locomotives would often be on-surface at weekends for a routine inspection. When the locomotives travelled up the 'drift' for repairs and maintenance, they had to be attached to the haulage rope and be hauled up at slow speed, in accordance with Transport Rule 6 (a local NCB rule). The rules also stipulated that no other vehicles could be attached to the haulage rope at that time. Haulage was by a Tredoman 50hp stationary engine which powered a 19mm diameter steel

rope - the maximum permissible weight was 25 tons at slow-speed haul. The operator of the haulage engine could communicate with the lower reaches of the mine (and vice versa) by means of a system of bell codes - when a locomotive was being brought out of the mine the bell code was '4-3', meaning, in mining terminology, 'slow outbye' (i.e. locomotive coming out slowly).

The branch line
As mentioned earlier, most of the coal from Park Mill Colliery was despatched from the screens adjacent to Clayton West station. They were connected to the standard gauge branch line and, as far as can be determined, coal wagons were initially marshalled there by the branch locomotives. Siding accommodation was provided alongside the signal box at Clayton West Junction for coal wagons to and from both of the collieries on the branch. The branch itself was latterly worked by electric token, with signal boxes at the junction and at Clayton West station. In the 1950s Fowler 2-6-4Ts worked the passenger trains, while the diesel era saw DMUs take over the service on 2 November 1959; the coal trains were usually handled by Class 37s and Class 40s.

Later years
Emley Moor Colliery achieved a degree of fame and a unique place in Yorkshire mining history by becoming the last major pit where the coal was 'handfilled' - i.e. the miners cut the coal manually by means of pick and shovel, and shovelled it from the face to the conveyor. The colliery's Beeston seam was of such high quality (with only three or four per cent ash content, and traditionally much prized by the steel industry at Sheffield, only twenty miles away), that it was perfectly economic to extract the coal in the old-fashioned way. The miners went down the shaft at Emley Moor and walked to the coal face through a part

of the mine known as 'Nine Clogs' - according to an ancient local story this section of the mine was originally developed by five men, one of whom had a peg leg, hence only nine clogs.

After World War II, Emley Moor Colliery produced an average of 2,500-3,500 tons of coal per week, and epic stories are told in the village about a Polish miner, one Marian Rockiki, who is reputed to have single-handedly shovelled forty tons of coal in one shift. Another famous miner was Reuben Kenworthy, who worked for thirty years at Emley Moor and whose personal record was thirty-three tons in a six-hour shift, with a lifetime average of twenty-two tons. Mr.Kenworthy was featured in a television programme in the 1980s, and became the Yorkshire coalfield's oldest handfiller. Asked about his labours, the modest 5ft 2in tall Mr.Kenworthy stated '...it was just a day's work...' and was '...all a matter of pacing and technique...'.

Emley Moor's last handfilling face was known as the Beeston y20s Seam, where a typical work-cycle was as follows... The 'boring shift' came on duty in the afternoon and excavated a 5" deep hole under the length of the coal face 225 yards in length. Then, working for much of the time laid on their backs, they drilled up to eighty holes in the face using a compressed air drill. The night shift took over at 10pm and ensured that the roadways reached the working face and were satisfactorily enlarged. At 5.00am the dayshift came on duty and, after walking through Nine Clogs, arrived at the coal face. The ready-drilled shot holes were then 'stemmed' (explosive put in and the hole filled) and fired, before a team of sixteen handfillers slithered into the forest of pit props with their picks and shovels. These handfillers worked, with a

special wooden chock to support their back, and a piece of old carpet to protect their shoulder, in a seam which, in places, was only sixteen inches high - in other words, the width of these two pages! They worked with a steady rhythm - and a deft flick of their 14lb shovels - to transfer the coal on to a conveyor belt, which took it to the narrow gauge tub loading point; the tubs were later replaced by a conveyor belt to the surface. Each man shovelled a daily average of about twenty tons - this measure was known as a 'stint' - but it was not unknown to shovel a 'stint and a half' (30 tons), or even a 'double stint' (40 tons). It was essential for each man to complete at least his daily 'stint', as bonus wages were paid for any excess production. Other workmen below ground operated the tramways which carried ready-cut pit props, timber bars, chocks, and steel arches, etc. In the 1970s the coal was still prized by the steel industry, although much of it was then exported to Sweden.

In the late 1970s the NCB Barnsley Area announced a major reorganisation whereby a considerable sum of money was to be spent on the redevelopment of the coal preparation plant at Woolley Colliery at Darton (to the east of Park Mill and Emley Moor). The scheme involved several local mines despatching their coal by means of underground roadways to Woolley for washing, grading and despatch. Park Mill Colliery was part of the scheme, and in April 1981 the last train of coal left the screens to be taken away down the branch line. By May 1981 rail traffic had ceased altogether at Park Mill, and there were no wagons left on site. The weigh cabin was boarded up, and there were massive stockpiles of coal along the side of the screens and all over the standard gauge

rails. Hudswell Clarke W/No.D1094 was stored beneath the screens, although not for long, as things turned out - it was transferred to Gascoigne Wood Colliery near Selby *circa* July 1981. It moved to Hartwood Exports Ltd of Birdwell, Barnsley, in April 1982. Park Mill's coal was thereafter sent - as had been intended - underground to Woolley.

At Emley Moor, coal continued to be washed at Skelmanthorpe screens and despatched by rail. However, rail use declined rapidly during the early 1980s, and soon ceased altogether, with all Emley Moor coal subsequently being despatched by road. The branch line serving the two collieries, having lost all its freight traffic, could not hope to continue on the meagre income generated by passenger traffic, and so it came as little surprise when closure was announced. This was effected on Monday 24 January 1983 and, after the last train had passed, Clayton West and Skelmanthorpe stations put up their shutters for good.

In April 1983 Emley Moor Colliery was partly mechanised, with the first power loader being installed in the newly developed and thicker Whinmoor seam. A few handfillers were retained (including Mick Craven, at only 21 years of age the youngest of the breed), and so the old and new methods continued alongside each other for a while. However, the retention of the old methods came in for criticism from none other than Reuben Kenworthy, who opined that '...no-one should really be doing this sort of work in this day and age'

Emley Moor's staff of 290 was reduced to 230, enabling some men (including Mr.Kenworthy) to take voluntary redundancy. The workforce was further reduced to 216 men by the start of the 1984/85

The brick-built engine shed at Skelmanthorpe Screens on 22 May 1979, with the diesel fuel tank clearly visible on the roof. As related in the text, this building was, in effect, a pair of single-road sheds back to back and separated by a wall. One engine fitted neatly into each half of the shed. PHOTOGRAPH: ADRIAN BOOTH

A fine portrait of STANDBACK No.2 in steam near Skelmanthorpe Screens on 31 August 1967. The locomotive's lettering - including 'NCB' on the cab side - and the lining on the cab are clearly seen. Despite extensive enquiries, we have been unable to determine the significance of the name STANDBACK - enlightenment would be welcome. PHOTOGRAPH: ROGER MONK

miners strike. Two underground roadways collapsed during the strike, prompting the NCB to announce that there was only one year's coal left at the colliery. In fact, the new Whinmoor seam had proved to be very dirty, and was stated to have an ash content of over fifty per cent. The almost inevitable consequence of these factors was that the colliery was placed on the notorious closure 'hit-list'.

After the strike, the miners at Emley Moor considered that there was plenty of workable coal left in their colliery, and they announced that they were prepared to continue working it by the old traditional methods. A group of miners, led by pit deputy Trevor Tyas, hoped to be offered redundancy so that they could plough their money (about £10,000 per man) back into the colliery, which they intended to oper-

ate as a private company. They felt they had the expertise to work the 17-22 inch Beeston seam by the old methods - thereby avoiding the need for costly modern equipment - and produce about 500 tons of quality coal per week for sale to small merchants. Months of talks ensued with the NCB, but the men's plans were dashed by the NCB who refused permission, claiming the mine had no realistic reserves. The

Emley Moor's last steam locomotive was STANDBACK No.3 (Hudswell Clarke W/No.1817), which was fifteen years old when it arrived from Hartley Bank Colliery in February 1968. It was kept as cover for the Fowler diesel, and consequently spent much of its time standing in the yard near the shed, as evidenced on 24 August 1975. PHOTOGRAPH: ADRIAN BOOTH

Skelmanthorpe Screens on 2 July 1978, with John Fowler 0-4-0 diesel W/No.22075 prominent. A number of wagons, some steel bodied, other wooden, stand in the yard The conical structure is a washing plant, and large stockpiles of coal are visible in the distance on the extreme right. PHOTOGRAPH: ADRIAN BOOTH

local M.P. John Whitfield took a different viewpoint, claiming the NCB was determined to close the mine but ensure that no one else was allowed to work it. The NCB won the day - as so often happened at the time - and Emley Moor Colliery was formally closed on Friday 20 December 1985. This marked the end of some 600 years of mining at Emley.

Rail traffic had officially ceased at Skelmanthorpe screens in January 1980 - with the closure of the Clayton West branch - although some coal was thereafter stockpiled on the site of the screens and later taken away by road. Some track was lifted at this time, and all the internal user wooden wagons were scrapped. Thomas Hill W/No 158c was placed in the

shed for storage; the building had not been used since 1900, from which time the locomotive always had stood out in the yard or under the screens. It was sold to C.F.Booth Ltd of Rotherham and left the site in February 1984; they resold it to Roe Brothers Ltd, who moved it to their Sheffield scrapyard on 10 March 1984 and used it as their yard shunter. The Skelmanthorpe

John Fowler 0-4-0 diesel-mechanical shunter W/No.22075 gave over forty years continuous service at Skelmanthorpe Screens. It was not the most beautiful of locomotives, but had plenty of character, as evidenced in this photograph which was taken in the north yard on 17 July 1974. The locomotive's nameplate, IRVING, is on the side of the cab. PHOTOGRAPH: ADRIAN BOOTH

Thomas Hill W/No.158c of 1965 was a 179hp diesel-hydraulic, painted green and numbered TL39. It was in the yard at Skelmanthorpe Screens on 22 May 1979, standing beside a disused wooden-bodied internal user wagon. PHOTOGRAPH: ADRIAN BOOTH

screens were demolished in 1986 and, by November that year, the engine shed had been reduced to a pile of bricks; all the sidings had been lifted, as had the BR branch. The Emley Moor Colliery headgears were dismantled, and these days the site is a small industrial estate.

Meanwhile, at Park Mill Colliery, it was a slightly different story. The colliery was upgraded underground in the late 1970s/early 1980s for the Woolley scheme, with the coal being taken to Woolley by means of modern bogie mine cars built by Gyro Mining Transport Ltd (usually known

as GMT). Park Mill continued working into the 1980s and even found minor sources of other income - for example, a training centre gave instruction to local miners, while the engine shed facility was used to overhaul locomotives from other collieries. On 8 January 1983 two narrow gauge 28hp

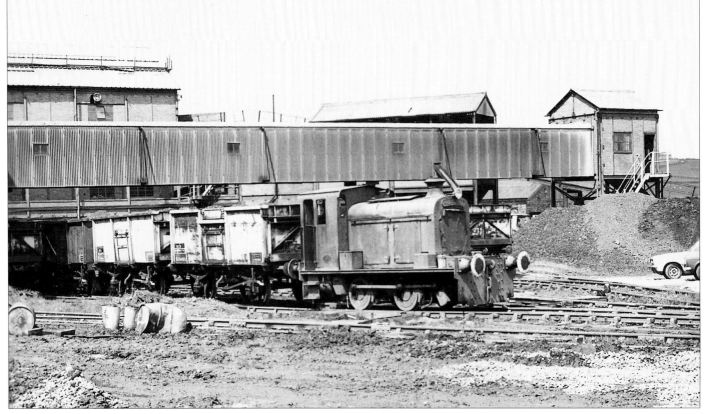

Hudswell Clarke W/No.D1094 was a tiny locomotive, being of only 72hp. The NCB purchased it to shunt occasional traffic at their Shafton Central Workshops at Barnsley, but it was later found to be ideal for the relatively light duties at Park Mill Colliery. It was at work, shunting a rake of 16-ton mineral wagons, at the screens on 22 May 1979. PHOTOGRAPH: ADRIAN BOOTH

John Fowler W/No.22075 at Skelmanthorpe Screens on 8 October 1978. PHOTOGRAPH: ADRIAN BOOTH

The narrow gauge engine shed at Park Mill Colliery, seen on the misty morning of Saturday 12 January 1980, with 2ft 6in gauge Hudswell Clarke W/No.DM1356, formerly named DEBORAH, outside. The start of the 1 in 12 'drift' - the 'passageway' taking the railway underground - is on the right, the entrance being protected by ornate-topped gates which were locked when the mine was not operating. The mist just enabled the photograph to be taken, but was thick enough to cause the photographer consternation that the afternoon's Huddersfield Town v Lincoln City match could be postponed. Fortunately, though, the game was played, and resulted in a 3-2 home win. PHOTOGRAPH: ADRIAN BOOTH

4-wheel diesel hydraulic locomotives arrived from Kinsley Colliery, south-east of Wakefield; these were Hunslet W/Nos.8831 and 8832 which had been delivered new to Kinsley in 1978 but had never been used there. They had been left on the surface, out in the open, for over four years and, not surprisingly, their bodywork had become very tarnished and their engines were seized up. The engineering staff at Park Mill were given the task of renovating the pair, before transferring them to Redbrook Colliery at Barnsley for surface duties. W/No.8831 went to its new home in August 1985 and W/No.8832 followed in March 1986. In October 1985 Hunslet W/No.6631 of 1965 - which carried a worksplate showing it to be of 29hp, arrived from Dodworth Colliery near Barnsley. It was to be overhauled and re-gauged to 2ft 0in for use at Barnsley Main Colliery but, although it was regauged (with great difficulty), the project was not completed and the loco was

Rail traffic ceased at Park Mill screens in April 1981, and when the site was visited a few weeks later - on 16 May - coal was stockpiled, windows were broken, and redundant Hudswell Clarke W/No.D1094 was stabled under the screens (it can just be seen on the third screen road from the left). The locomotive was, however, later transferred to Gascoine Wood Colliery for further duties. PHOTOGRAPH: ADRIAN BOOTH

One hundred years after the Clayton West branch opened in 1879 it was still carrying coal traffic. Class 37 diesel No.37067 enters Skelmanthorpe station on 22 May 1979, bound for Clayton West Junction with a train of loaded coal wagons from Park Mill Colliery. PHOTOGRAPH: ADRIAN BOOTH

scrapped in 1990. Park Mill Colliery was officially merged with Denby Grange Colliery at Netherton in December 1988, but the new arrangements were short-lived as Park Mill closed in June 1989. The 'drift' - the passageway - which took the narrow gauge railway underground was filled in,

the gantry across the main road (for years a familiar local landmark) was taken down, and the headgears and other buildings demolished. Of the underground locomotives at Park Mill, Hudswell Clarke W/Nos.DM747 and DM890 had already departed, having been transferred to Prince

of Wales Colliery at Pontefract in December 1985. The colliery's closure prompted the donation of W/Nos.DM746, DM748 and DM1356 to the Yorkshire Mining Museum, Caphouse, Wakefield. The trio moved to their new home (thus signalling the end of locomotives at Emley Moor and

Springwood Shaft (grid reference SE270128) was alongside the A636 road, just to the north-east of Clayton West, and part of the Park Mill Colliery. It was used for men and materials only, though it was also available as an emergency exit in case of disaster. No coal was wound there. The site was photographed on 15 November 1986, but is now closed and the buildings and headgear have been demolished. PHOTOGRAPH: ADRIAN BOOTH

Park Mill collieries) on 24 August 1990.

These days, Emley Moor is principally known for its famous television mast. The original tubular mast (which was not insured) collapsed on 19 March 1969, and was replaced by a 900 feet high concrete tower, surmounted by a 180 feet mast. Fame was brought to the parish during the 1997/98 football season when non-league Emley F.C. fought their way through to the third round of the F.A.Cup, being narrowly defeated by West Ham United of the Premier League.

On a more railway orientated front, Clayton West station is now the base of the Kirklees Light Railway, a 1ft 3in gauge line which commenced operations in October 1991. The KLR has three steam locomotives, one 'steam outline' petrol locomotive and one diesel. They have their own engine shed at Clayton West, where the station buildings have been renovated. In December 1992 the KLR extended its line to Skelmanthorpe.

Author's note: My principal sources were Mining and Quarrying in the Huddersfield District *by D.H.Holmes (Huddersfield Tolson Memorial Museum, 1967),* Pennine Journey *by William B. Stocks (The Advertiser Press, Huddersfield, 1958),* The Huddersfield & Sheffield Junction Railway *by Martin Bairstow (1985), and* A History of Denby Dale Urban District *(D.D.U.D.C, 1974). Thanks to Judith Hodge at Huddersfield Library who kindly located references in local newspapers, to Mike Swift and Bob Darvill who both helped to resolve some of my specific queries, and to Jim Peden.*

A final look at Emley Moor Colliery's Skelmanthorpe screens, this time on 16 May 1981. By this date the screens were little used - indeed, no wagons are visible in the yard. PHOTOGRAPH: ADRIAN BOOTH

This pile of scrap metal used to be John Fowler diesel locomotive W/No.22075. It was cut up in the yard at Skelmanthorpe screens on 22 May 1979 and the pieces were collected two days later by scrap merchants Bush of Alfreton. PHOTOGRAPH: ADRIAN BOOTH

BELVOIR JUNCTION
Portrait of a country junction

Words and pictures by David Pearce

A view of Belvoir Junction in the down direction - i.e. looking westwards towards Nottingham - across frosted tracks on 1 January 1980, almost a year and a half after the Denton branch was finally closed. The branch can be seen diverging beyond the signal box, behind the shunters/platelayers' hut. The line in the foreground is the down refuge siding leading into the down spur which is beyond the branch junction. The refuge siding could accommodate 80 wagons, and engine and brake, but the caveat in the WTT Appendix stated that: *'Guards and Shunters responsible for stabling trains in this siding must ensure that wagons are not left in such a position as to cause any obstruction to the public footpath level crossing or interfere with the view from, or the means of access to, the adjacent signal box. A space equal to 15 wagon lengths must be left clear in front of the signal box'.*

The tortuously titled Ambergate, Nottingham & Boston & Eastern Junction Railway Company opened its line between Nottingham (Colwick Junction) and Grantham on 15 July 1850. The line was worked under contract, initially by E.B.Wilson & Co and later by Messrs.Neale & Wilson of Grantham, but on 31 March 1852 a working agreement was sealed with the Great Northern Railway. When the GNR main line reached Grantham on 1 August 1852, a through service (worked by the GNR) was advertised between London and Nottingham, running via Grantham and the AN&B&EJR, but this rather displeased the Midland Railway who had hitherto had a monopoly at Nottingham. This gave rise to one of the famous railway incidents of the period: when the GNR's inaugural through train from London arrived at Nottingham, the Midland Railway forced the locomotive into the old Midland Counties shed at Nottingham and disconnected the rails, thus effectively holding the engine hostage. Matters were, however, eventually resolved, and on 2 April 1855 the AN&B&EJR was formally leased to the GNR. Somewhat superfluously, perhaps, in May 1860 the AN&B&EJR changed its corporate title to the Nottingham & Grantham Railway & Canal Company.

During those formative years of the Nottingham-Grantham line, iron ore deposits were discovered in the area, particularly in and around Belvoir, to the south of the railway, but it was another twenty years or so before the ore was extracted on a commercial scale. As the local mining industry developed the local railway network expanded accordingly, various mineral and freight-orientated lines being opened in the 1870s and 1880s by the Great Northern and its once unneighbourly neighbour, the Midland Railway.

One of the Great Northern's mineral lines served the Denton area on the Belvoir estate, where the Stanton Ironworks Company had obtained leases to work the ironstone. The mineral line diverged from the Nottingham-Grantham line a little under 1½ miles to the east of Bottesford station (at the appropriately titled Belvoir Junction) and headed in a generally southerly direction towards Denton. Although the main line was only leased by the Great Northern, the mineral branch was wholly Great Northern property. The first section of the branch opened in 1883 - this section was 2 miles 60 chains in length and terminated at a wharf on the Grantham Canal at Woolsthorpe (at a point originally referred to as Bottesford Siding, later

Woolsthorpe Sidings). A GNR engineer's report indicates that the first load of iron ore was dispatched from Bottesford (Woolsthorpe) siding to Belvoir Junction on 29 June 1883, but an alternative date is suggested by the late Eric Tonks in his definitive work *The Ironstone Railways and Tramways of the Midlands*; Tonks states that the first ore was dispatched from Bottesford Siding on 3 August 1883, being taken down to Belvoir Junction by a contractor's locomotive (Neilson 0-4-0ST W/ No.1941).

In 1885 the branch was extended southwards by a distance of 2 miles 71 chains to Denton Sidings (the sidings were, in fact, about mid-way between the villages of Denton and Harston). A GNR engineer's report dated 2 March 1886 implies that the extension was, at that time, worked, not by GNR locomotives, but by locomotives belonging to the Stanton Ironworks Co.

The branch and its siding facilities were upgraded at various times, but the most significant changes were seen in 1941 when new connections and exchange facilities were provided 3 miles 54 chains along the branch to serve a major new quarry at Harlaxton. This quarry had its own standard gauge railway to bring the ironstone down to the exchange point on the Denton

The Denton branch as it approaches Belvoir Junction - this view looks north, with the bridge across the A52 road in the foreground. The check rail gives an indication of the tightness of the curve. From left to right beyond the shrubbery is the Nottingham-Grantham railway line with Belvoir Junction signal box in the distance. Branch trains were subject to a permanent speed restriction of 20mph. This picture was taken on 1 January 1980.

branch (see *Railway Bylines* magazine, Vol.3 No.8).

The Denton branch incorporated some fairly steep gradients as it climbed southwards away from Belvoir Junction, there being sections of 1 in 80, 1 in 70 and even 1 in 57. Loaded trains descended towards the junction. It was not unknown for

breakaways to occur, the last reported incident being on 17 June 1972 when twenty-two empty mineral wagons broke away from an ascending train, ran back along the branch and derailed on an embankment near Belvoir.

The branch was never envisaged as a passenger carrying line - it spent its life as

an archetypal mineral line. That said, the sidings at Belvoir Junction, Woolsthorpe, Welby (56 chains from the end of the branch) and Denton were available for the handling of public goods traffic, these public facilities being nominally retained until 14 June 1965; it is known that a small amount of general goods, principally agri-

Looking north along the Denton branch with the branch distant signal prominent.

A close-up of the branch distant, a former GN somersault signal on a concrete post, still reasonably intact eighteen months after the Denton branch's final closure.

cultural produce, was once handled at the sidings, though from the 1920s onwards the Working Timetables make no mention of any general goods workings on the branch. The branch was worked on the 'one engine in steam' principle, latterly 'one train working', which, of course, allowed for only one train on the branch at a time. The train staff for possession of the branch was kept in the signal box at Belvoir Junction.

The signal box at Belvoir Junction broke up the section between Sedgebrook 'box, 1 mile 32 chains to the east, and Bottesford station 'box, 1 mile 36 chains to the west, on the Nottingham-Grantham line. Belvoir Junction 'box had opened on 7 October 1875 - i.e. some eight years before the Denton branch was constructed - and had originally been known simply as Belvoir. The 'box originally had a Saxby & Farmer 5 frame, but this was replaced in 1885 by a Saxby & Farmer 4" rocker frame.

Belvoir Junction itself faced west (i.e. towards Nottingham), as the principal destination for the ironstone was Stanton Ironworks, between Nottingham and

The Denton branch closed in February 1974, was reopened in April 1976, but closed - this time for good - in July 1978. So, when visited on 2 January 1975, the branch and its junction with the main line were in limbo. This view looks east towards Grantham. From the left we have the up refuge siding, the up main, the down main, and then the down spur. There were no facing connections from either of the main lines to the branch - as the accompanying diagram shows, access to the branch from either main line required a reversal. Consequently, empties from the Nottingham direction arriving on the up main had to reverse across on to the down main or down spur and then draw forward on to the branch just beyond the telegraph poles; hence the 'dods' in the foreground to allow movement straight ahead or on to the branch.

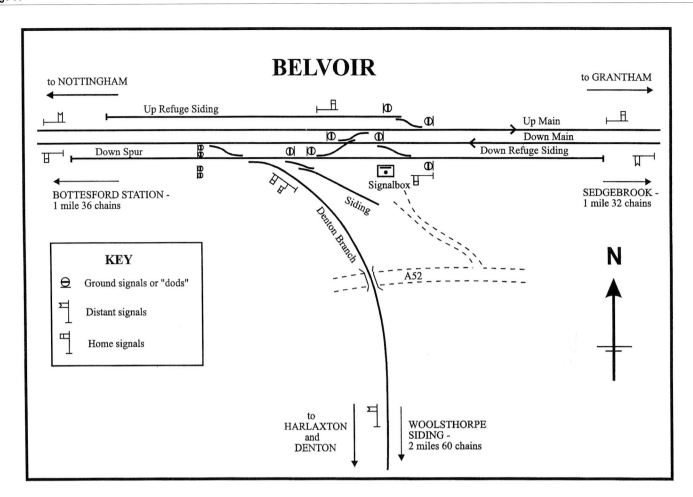

BELVOIR

to NOTTINGHAM

Up Refuge Siding

Up Main

Down Main

Down Refuge Siding

Down Spur

Signalbox

Siding

Denton Branch

to GRANTHAM

BOTTESFORD STATION -
1 mile 36 chains

SEDGEBROOK -
1 mile 32 chains

A52

KEY

⊖ Ground signals or "dods"

Distant signals

Home signals

N

to
HARLAXTON
and
DENTON

WOOLSTHORPE
SIDING -
2 miles 60 chains

In the foreground is the up refuge siding, capable of holding fifty-five wagons, an engine and a brake. Across the two main lines, the Denton branch curves away southwards on a gradient; the branch home signal on the right protected the down main line, and the small bracket signal attached to the main post permitted shunting in to the down spur. The date is 2 January 1975.

A rear view of Belvoir Junction signal box, taken on 1 January 1980 from the vehicle park at the end of the lane leading up from the A52. The position of the chimney suggests that the stove was in the back corner of the 'box, farthest from the door, and undoubtedly a welcome sight on a cold winter's day. The rear window gave a view of the progress of trains on the branch. In the mid-1960s Belvoir Junction 'box was manned on a two-shift basis - 6am to 2pm and 2pm to 10pm - and was switched out overnight and on Sundays.

The signal box with its associated lamp hut to the left; between the 'box and the lamp hut is the 'stockaded' coal bunker storing fuel for the stove. The decorative bargeboards and finials at each end of the signal box roof are repeated in miniature on the roof of the toilet perched on the end of the balcony, even though the toilet was a later addition. The ground signal on the extreme right is for exit from the up refuge siding, and the one just to the right of the 'box gives access from the up main to the down lines via the crossover. This picture was taken on 2 January 1975.

Derby; there was also a trailing connection to the down line. The Stanton traffic was worked by engines and crews from Colwick - there were usually several trains each day, Mondays to Saturdays - the trains being worked by almost anything Colwick had available, though O2 and O4 2-8-0s, B1 4-6-0s and J6 0-6-0s, and latterly Ivatt and BR Class 4 2-6-0s, were fairly common. In later years there were daily workings from Denton to Scunthorpe, and these required interesting manoeuvres at Belvoir Junction to enable the trains to 'reverse' and head east.

Despite - or possibly because of - the Denton branch's status as a mineral line, it did not escape the attention of enthusiasts' specials. One of the last was the 'Kesteven Ironstone Branches Railtour' which was run by the RCTS on Saturday 15 April 1972 - the party's two-car DMU traversed the entire length of the Denton branch.

The Denton branch ceased operations in 1973, the demand for iron and steel having fallen to a level where extraction from the Belvoir area was no longer an economic proposition. However, the branch was not officially closed until 15 February 1974; with the formal closure of the branch, the signal box at Belvoir Junction was 'mothballed' (or 'permanently switched out', at it was officially described) on the same date. The 'box had, incidentally, been equipped with a new Westinghouse 17A frame containing 26 levers on 8 September 1963.

Despite the closure of the branch, a visit to Belvoir Junction on 2 January 1975 revealed that everything was still intact,

though the Denton line and its associated sidings were gently rusting. But, as things turned out, the branch was to have a new lease of life. Before very long, ironstone working was soon resumed at Harlaxton, and on 28 April 1976 the Denton branch reopened as far as Casthorpe Junction (near the old Grantham Canal, some 2¾ miles from Belvoir Junction) so that the ironstone could be taken by rail to Bilston in the West Midlands and Shelton at Stoke-on-Trent. However, the reprieve was not long-lived as, in 1977, the British Steel Corporation revised their operations at Shelton and this effectively killed off the outlet for Harlaxton ore. Traffic on the Denton branch ceased again in September 1977 (latterly there had been about one train each week) and the branch was formally closed, this time for good, in July 1978. Belvoir Junction signal box was officially closed on 7 January 1979.

The lifting of the branch commenced in late October 1979, and a visit to Belvoir Junction a couple of months or so later - on 1 January 1980 - revealed that all the signals had been removed and the points disconnected. The signal box nameboards had gone and some track had been removed. However, the distant signal for the branch was still *in situ* in the gentle cutting just south of the bridge over the A52 road. By 27 May 1980 the signal box was still standing, though most of the track associated with the Denton branch had been removed, with the exception of the up refuge siding, the down spur and the points on the main lines. The 'box was, however, subsequently demolished and the bridge over the A52 was swept away by road improvements in

connection with the Bottesford by-pass. The Nottingham-Grantham lines were, of course, untouched, as the line remained open. It is still with us today, though rail passengers passing the site of Belvoir Junction nowadays would be hard pressed to identify any real hint of the once thriving mineral line which came in from the south.

Contributor's note: *Thanks are due to Mr. Roger Newman of the Signalling Record Society for making available information about Belvoir Junction signal box.*

Above. **A general view looking westwards towards Nottingham taken on 2 January 1975 from the foot crossing. The Denton branch can just be seen on the extreme left behind the signal box. The main crossover in the middle of the picture was important, not only for providing access from the up main line to the branch, but also as an outlet for loaded trains heading eastwards. The up home signal on the right is in the off position as the signal box is switched out - it had been taken out of use when the Denton branch closed (for the first time) in February 1974.**

A closer view of the junction, looking east towards Grantham. The track immediately to the right of the hut was the public delivery siding, but had latterly been used as a 'lie' for brake vans. This picture was taken on 1 January 1980 after the signalling had been removed.

The shunters/platelayers alongside the delivery siding, 1 January 1980.

The South Western Pottery's Peckett 'W4' 0-4-0ST, appropriately named GEORGE JENNINGS, was kept in excellent condition; when this picture was taken at the pottery on 30 April 1957, the locomotive was fifty-five years old. PHOTOGRAPH: AUSTIN ATTEWELL; COURTESY HUGH DAVIES

THE SOUTH WESTERN POTTERY
George Jennings of Poole

by Paul Webb

In 1856, George Jennings established the South Western Pottery at Parkstone in Dorset - there was a seam of Dorset ball clay in the immediate vicinity, hence the choice of location. Jennings already had a pottery in the Lambeth area of London, and although Thomas Wragg & Sons Ltd of Swadlincote took over the Jennings Company in 1903, the Jennings name continued at Parkstone until the closure of the works in 1967. The buildings at Parkstone were believed to have been constructed with bricks from a brickworks on the Lilliput Road nearby.

The pottery

George Jennings' South Western Pottery was situated about ½-mile or so to the south of Parkstone station at Map Reference SZ037908. From 1860 onwards, the pottery specialised in terracotta work, including sanitary pipework and acid resisting pipework, some of which was used in the nearby Holton Heath Cordite Factory.

In this undated picture, GEORGE JENNINGS waits close to the yard at Parkstone station. We see further evidence that the railway staff at the pottery took considerable pride in the locomotive. PHOTOGRAPH: FRANK JONES

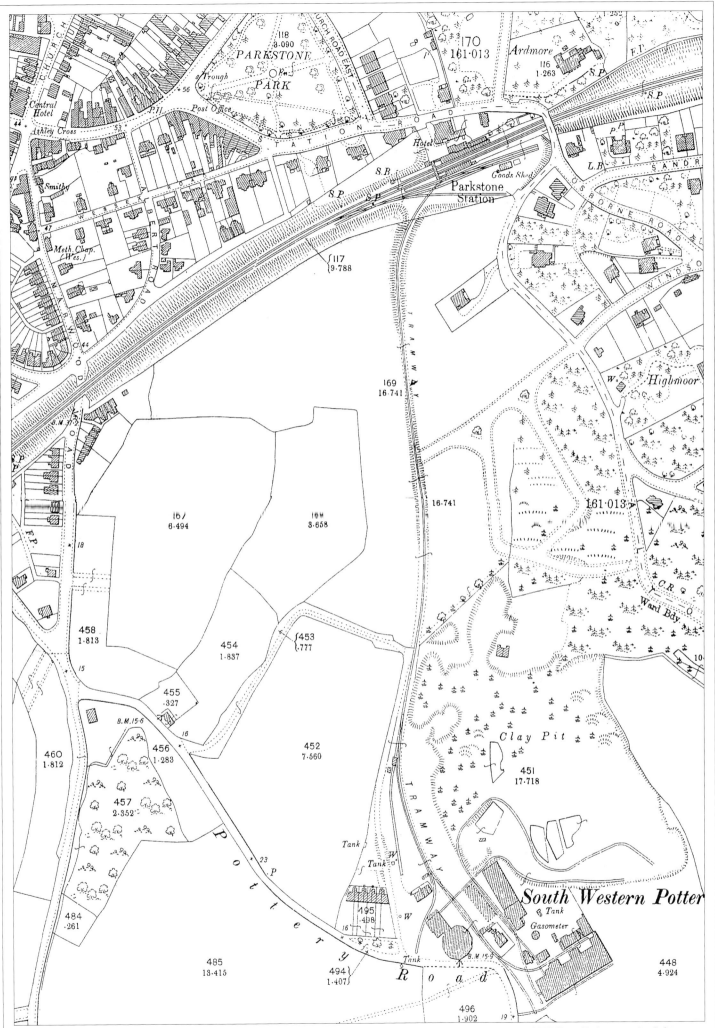

The 25" Ordnance Survey map of 1902 shows the contemporary railway set-up at the South Western Pottery and the connection to the L&SWR line at Parkstone station. In later years the pottery tramway was extended southwards to Salterns Pier at Poole Harbour, though that extension was comparatively short-lived, being lifted before 1928. Please note that this map has been slightly reduced from its original scale. CROWN COPYRIGHT

GEORGE JENNINGS

(Proprietors: Thos. Wragg & Sons, Ltd.)

South Western Pottery

PARKSTONE, POOLE, Dorset

Telegrams:
Jennings, Parkstone

Telephones:
Parkstone Nos. 507 & 508

London Office:

Albany Buildings, 39 Victoria St., Westminster, S.W.1

Telegrams: Kelpware, Victoria, London   Telephone: Abbey 2801

Manufacturers of the
**CELEBRATED POOLE STONEWARE PIPES AND
FITTINGS, FIRE BRICKS, SINKS, Etc.**

Specialities:

**STONEWARE PIPES WITH ACID RESISTING QUALITIES
TO BRITISH STANDARD SPECIFICATIONS 1143 & 784**

PLEASE QUOTE CATALOGUE NUMBERS
WHEN ORDERING

An early catalogue of George Jennings wares include drain pipes and gullies, air bricks, and stoneware filter-bed tiles. Many of Jennings' production methods and much of his machinery were considered rather advanced - he was respected as being 'ahead of his field' - and he took out patents on a number of his products. Bricks were also manufactured at an adjacent site in a Hoffman continuous brick kiln (this is shown on the accompanying maps), but the kiln was dismantled in 1939. In 1930 the first British continuous tunnel kiln producing salt glazed pipes was developed, and during the 1930s this kiln produced large quantities of sanitary pipes and fittings; it was, however, not used after 1939. The kiln was built by Messrs. Shaws, and is also shown on the map.

Most of the fittings produced by Jennings at Parkstone were hand moulded, exactly the same methods being used from 1856 right up to closure in 1967. The procedure was to use a plaster of Paris mould in two halves - a skilled moulder could tell by feel when he had laid in a even thickness of clay in the mould. The straight pipe sections were made by extruding through a die a mixture of raw clay and 'grog' (a mix

Left. The title page from the pottery company's catalogue.

Below. A row of kilns at the South Western Pottery, 30 April 1957. PHOTOGRAPH: AUSTIN ATTEWELL; COURTESY HUGH DAVIES

Right. The 'large kiln', showing more closely the steel bands around the masonry. PHOTOGRAPH: AUSTIN ATTEWELL, COURTESY HUGH DAVIES

of broken fired clay, ground up and mixed to a slurry). In the early days, loose couplers were used to join the sections of pipe together - these couplers were made separately from the pipes themselves. Later on, the practice was for the pipes to have 'built-in' sockets - the socket was formed first, then the rest of the pipe was formed by extruding around a central mandrel. In more recent years the straight pipes were formed and the sockets hand finished although, these days, modern clayware drain pipes of 9" diameter or less have reverted to the method of separate couplers. Unfired or 'green' pipes were left to dry before firing; there were hydraulic lifts between the floors in the old terracotta works, and a system of small trolleys, known as 'Dandies' were used to move the heavy 'green' pipes and fittings around on the floors.

The kilns were coal fired, and the pipes were sealed inside and the kiln heated to around 800°C until free from all moisture. The temperature was then increased to 1100°C and salt was added to the fires - the salt vaporised, coated and glazed the pipes, which were by then white hot. The pipes, when cooled, were later pressure-tested to ensure they were of satisfactory quality.

The machinery at the plant was steam powered. In 1922 a 125kw AC alternator manufactured by Newtons of Derby was installed; it was driven by a 600hp single-cylinder steam engine manufactured by Messrs.Thornewall and Warham of Burton-on-Trent. The cylinder was 24" diameter x 42" stroke, had Corliss type valve gear, a 12-foot flywheel, with a belt-drive

formed of 20 cotton ropes each of 1½" diameter. In 1930 a new 75kw AC alternator, manufactured by Crompton Parkinson of Chelmsford, was installed; it was powered by a 50hp Bellis and Morcom twin-cylinder vertical engine. This machine provided power for the lighting and the tunnel kiln twenty-four hours a day. In the pottery's final years of operations, some of the steam-driven machinery was modified so as to be electrically driven.

The railway system - standard gauge

George Jennings' pottery was connected to the L&SWR (later SR) main line at Parkstone station, four miles west of Bournemouth Central. A private standard gauge line diverged from the down (south) side of the station yard, running about ½-mile southward to the pottery - it was used to bring in coal to the pottery and, of course, to take away finished pottery items. It is known that the line was operational by 1872 as George Jennings purchased their first locomotive in that year (more of which anon), but it is unclear whether the line had been in situ prior to that date; if so, one assumes it was worked by horses.

At some time after 1902 the standard gauge was extended southwards to Salterns Pier, on the north-east side of Poole Harbour. The pier, which was made from timber and old brick and pipe rubble, was used for sea-borne exports of pottery products. The line to the pier was removed in 1928, and the pier itself later fell into disuse. Another standard gauge spur was also added at a later date - this spur looped around Parkstone Cemetery, crossed the main road and then followed the course of

Sandbanks Road to a site where, after World War I, railway wagons were repaired by Messrs.Alban Richards & Co.

The company employed a succession of three locomotives on the standard gauge lines, each new locomotive replacing its predecessor. All were outside-cylinder 0-4-0STs. The first was built by Fox Walker of Bristol in 1872 (W/No.159); it was sold to a contractor in 1893, having been replaced at Parkstone 1893 by Peckett XL class W/No.528 which was named GEORGE JENNINGS. (Pecketts were, of course, the successors of Fox Walker). In 1902 the Peckett was returned to the maker in part exchange for one of the firm's new W4 class locomotives (W/No.920) which inherited the name GEORGE JENNINGS from the engine it replaced. The first of Jennings' two Pecketts (W/No.528) was later resold to Hutchinson & Co, a firm of contractors with an address at Leek Brook in Staffordshire.

At the pottery, the locomotives were accommodated in a brick-built engine shed. It appears that repairs and overhauls were undertaken elsewhere - it is quite possible that some repairs were carried out at Peckctt's workshops in Bristol, though on 5 February 1949 GEORGE JENNINGS was observed at Bevois Park, Southampton, en route to G.P.Wilson & Sons of Northam for repair. GEORGE JENNINGS was employed at Parkstone until November 1963 when it was dispatched to Messrs.W.Turner; the intention was for the locomotive to be preserved, but it was scrapped by Turners in 1966.

SALT-GLAZED STONEWARE PIPES, BENDS, JUNCTIONS, ETC.

No. 25
Breeches

No. 26
Double Oblique

No. 27
Double Square

No. 28
Double Curved Square

No. 29
Double Curved Oblique

No. 30
Double Spaced
Oblique

No. 31
Double Curved
Oblique Junction
with Long Arms

No. 32
Curved Oblique
Junction
with Long Arm

GLAZED STONEWARE SLIPPER GULLIES

No. 123

The "Mansion" Slipper or Shoe is designed, in accordance with the model by-laws of the Local Government Board, to allow the waste pipes to discharge at least 18in. away from the trap.
Slipper is rebated to take a 22in. x 5in. wire cover or grid.

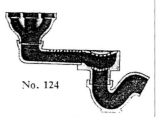

No. 124

The "Hospital." The triple Socket piece is for Bath and Lavatory Wastes. Connecting Shoe, Dish and Trap Socket Pieces are made in various sizes, as required.
Length of Shoe and Dish, 24in.

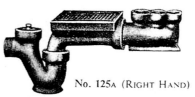

No. 125A (RIGHT HAND)

This Slipper is designed to receive separate Intake Pieces, which are provided with one or more inlets of the same or varying diameter to suit requirements. As the Intake Pieces discharge into the Slipper below the surface grating, any possibility of splashing is avoided. The trap being separate can be adjusted to any angle required, and can be supplied plain, or with inspection inlet and screw stopper as shown. This is made with Slipper part flush with wall and is therefore handed. Right hand No. 125A. Left hand No. 125B. Traps 4in. dia.

Intake Piece with two inlets. 2in. and 4in. dia. inlets

Intake Piece with one inlet. 2in. or 4in. dia. inlets

Cross Section of Slipper

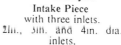

Intake Piece with three inlets. 2in., 3in. and 4in. dia. inlets.

Longitudinal Section of Slipper

The narrow gauge

The clay pits were connected to the pottery by a 2-foot gauge system. As was the usual practice, when the older pits were exhausted and new ones opened up, the tramway was repositioned accordingly. The early pits, incidentally, adjoined Pottery Road, while the later ones were a little to the north, above Mill Lane. Within the pits themselves, the tramway required repositioning far more frequently. The pits were quite deep and consequently the narrow gauge tramway climbed steeply out of them. This obviously restricted the number of wagons which could be hauled by the locomotives - usually, only one or two wagons could be hauled.

At Salterns Pier there was a short raised narrow gauge transhipment line linking the pier to the standard gauge line. This narrow gauge link was originally horse-worked, although there has been speculation that a locomotive might have been used.

Four different locomotives were used on the narrow gauge system at the clay pits. The first was a 4-wheeled petrol-mechanical Motor Rail Simplex with bow frames; its precise identity is uncertain, but it is known to have had served in France on the War Department Light Rail-way during World War I - as if to verify how close it had been to the action, it had shrapnel marks on its sides - and was purchased by Jennings' after the war. The Simplex was joined in 1930 by a new 4-wheeled petrol-mechanical Lister (W/No.3355), and in 1948 the stud of narrow gauge locomotives was increased to three with the arrival of a new 4-wheeled battery electric locomotive, manufactured by Victor Electrics Ltd (W/No.6712). A fourth narrow gauge locomotive was purchased new in 1956 - this was a 4-wheeled diesel-mechanical machine, built by F.Hibberd & Co (W/No.3790).

The Hibberd locomotive, although the newest, was sold to Thomas Ward Ltd. (of Ringwood, *not* Sheffield!) in 1965. The other three narrow gauge locomotives remained on site until 1966, although at least one of the three - the battery electric - had been out of use for many years.

As we have seen, the last standard gauge locomotive had been disposed of in 1966; the disposal of the three remaining narrow gauge locomotives in that same year confirms that, by then, George Jennings' railway operations had ceased. The tramway was lifted in 1967 and in the same year the works were put up for sale.

Acknowledgements: Much of the locomotive information was gleaned from the Industrial Railway Society's Handbook H, while some of the historical information about George Jennings' works came from the Poole Industrial Archaeology Group.

Above. **Examples of the South Western Pottery's wares, as advertised in the firm's catalogue.**

Top right. **A 2ft gauge tramway system connected the clay pits to the pottery, and there were eventually four locomotives nominally available for use on the tramway. The last of the four to arrive was Hibberd 'Planet' diesel-mechanical W/No.3790, which was purchased new in 1956. It was photographed shunting hopper wagons on 30 April 1957.**
PHOTOGRAPH: AUSTIN ATTEWELL; COURTESY HUGH DAVIES

Below right. **An interesting relic at the South Western Pottery was this elderly steam shovel, seen on 30 April 1957.**
PHOTOGRAPH: AUSTIN ATTEWELL; COURTESY HUGH DAVIES

THE SHROPSHIRE & MONTGOMERYSHIRE LIGHT RAILWAY
A miscellany
Photographs by Tim Shuttleworth

As explained in the April/May 1997 edition of *Railway Bylines* magazine, the Shropshire & Montgomeryshire Light Railway was taken over in 1941 by the War Department who established several military depots in the vicinity. Although the line went back to 'civvy street' in 1948 - being administered by the Western Region of the newly created British Railways - the WD retained a presence, albeit steadily reducing as the military depots closed one by one. Despite the Western Region administration, virtually all the train movements were WD workings. When an RCTS party visited the line on 25 April 1954, the special train was hauled by WD 'Austerity' 0-6-0ST No.167 and comprised two WD carriages and a brake van - the carriages were former LT&SR Ealing-Southend carriages which had had their original seats replaced by lengthwise wooden slatted seating; they were painted olive green and lettered S&M Lt.Rly R.E. Our upper photograph shows the RCTS train pausing at Ford, about halfway between Shrewsbury (Abbey) and Kinnerley Junction.

Befitting a 'Colonel Stephens' railway, the Shropshire & Montgomeryshire had a fair old hotch-potch of rolling stock and equipment. Several items remained on site long after the S&M itself had ceased operations; one such was the wooden baggage trailer which had been intended for use in conjunction with a Ford railcar set - the railcar set comprised two identical vehicles, and the idea was that the trailer would be positioned between the two. It is thought that the trailer was acquired at the same time as the railcars - in 1923 - but it seems to have been seldom used. Given the very nature of the trailer, and also its basic buffers and the drop-pin centre coupling (seen in the lower photograph), it is evident that there were few, if any, alternative duties to which it could be allocated. Nevertheless, although the railcars were scrapped in the early 1940s, the trailer lived on until at least the mid-1950s. This picture shows it on a siding at Kinnerley Junction on 25 April 1954.

By the time this picture was taken on 25 April 1954, the old S&M yard crane at Shrewsbury Abbey station had been in a semi-derelict condition for some time. However, some forty-five years on, and the crane still survives; it is now in private ownership at a site near Mountford Bridge, Shrewsbury.

The only Dowlais-built locomotive to make the move to Cardiff East Moors was 'C1' class 0-4-0T No.39, which duly became No.5. It is seen at East moors in April 1950, not too long before its withdrawal. Note the square-profile cab - a marked contrast to the 'D' class locomotives in the other photographs. PHOTOGRAPH: FRANK JONES

THE DOWLAIS GIANTS
The locomotives built at Dowlais Iron Works
by Haydn Watkins

The giants of Dowlais - the locomotives built at the Ifor Works of Guest Keen & Nettlefolds Ltd between 1906 and 1920 - represented a high point in that company's long involvement with the steam locomotive. This involvement originated in 1831 when steam as a form of motive power was still in its infancy, and when experimentation, combined with a necessary element of trial and error, was the order of the day.

It is widely known that the transportation of coal dominated the economic thinking of railways serving South Wales in the second half of the nineteenth century. However, the initial pressures to establish railways in the region came, not from coal interests, but from the ironmasters of the Merthyr/Dowlais area. The Glamorganshire Canal had been completed in 1794 and had served local industries well, but by the late 1820s it was considered inadequate to cope with the increased output from Merthyr's four ironworks - namely the Penydarren, Cyfartha, Plymouth and Dowlais Works. The opening of the 9½-mile Penydarren Tramroad from Merthyr to Abercynon in 1802 had done little to alleviate the problem since the tramroad still linked up with the canal, albeit closer to the Cardiff end of the journey.

Thus, one of the area's leading industrialists, John Josiah Guest, petitioned for a railway from Merthyr to Cardiff. The new company, the Taff Vale Railway Company, was incorporated on 21 June 1836 and the first section from Cardiff to Abercynon was completed in 1840. The extension to Merthyr was completed in 1841 and an incline to serve John Guest's ironworks at Dowlais was eventually finished in 1851.

John Guest, who became the first M.P. for Merthyr under the provisions of the 1832 Reform Act, also became the first chairman of the Taff Vale Railway.

Since 1815 the importance of the man and the importance of the iron company's fortunes had been inseparable. In that year John Guest had become managing partner, holding nine of the sixteen shares. At that time Dowlais had five furnaces in blast and was producing 15,600 tons of iron annually. In 1821 the ironworks started to produce rails for the Stockton & Darlington Railway, and in 1844 the company fulfilled a contract to supply 30,000 tons of rails to the Russian Railways, rapidly followed by a further order for 50,000 tons. By 1845 Dowlais was the largest ironworks in the world, covering an area of 40 acres, employing some 7,300 persons, and producing over 88,000 tons of iron per year.

For a company with such a massive output and an equally massive demand for raw materials, the need for an effective

The first locomotive to be wholly constructed at Dowlais was 0-6-0T ARTHUR KEEN, which was completed in January 1906. As evidenced here, it was a very smart-looking machine which, in the appearance stakes, could have put many of its 'main line' contemporaries to shame. PHOTOGRAPH: FRANK JONES

TABLE ONE: Original dimensions of locococmotives built at Dowlais Iron Works

Class	Type	Gauge	Total built	Cylinders	Wheel diameter	Boiler pressure	Weight (full)
A	0-6-0T	Standard	1	18" x 26" (i)	4' 3"	180lb	55t 0c
A1	0-6-0T	Standard	1	19" x 26" (i)	4' 0"	200lb	57t 10c
C1	0-4-0T	Standard	1	17½" x 22" (o)	3' 6"	175lb	42t 0c
D	0-4-0T	Standard	5	14" x 18" (i)	3' 6"	200lb	35t 0c
H	0-4-0T	3' 0"	1	10½" x 16" (o)		200lb	13t 10c

TABLE TWO: Summary of locomotives built at Dowlais Iron Works

No.	Name	Class	Built	Wdn.	Usual duties ‡
38	ARTHUR KEEN	A	1.1906	1938	Upper Branch
39	-	C1	2.1907	1950	Morlais limestone quarries; Ifor Works
40	KING GEORGE V	D	3.1907	*	Between blast furnaces and metal mixer
41	SANDYFORD	A1	4.1909	*	'Main line' traffic - upper to lower works
42	QUEEN MARY	D	5.1909	*	Between blast furnaces and metal mixer
43	-	D	6.1912	*	Shunting blast furnace bunkers
44	PANT	D	7.1914	*	Finished steel traffic
45	-	H	8.1917	*	Bessemer plant
46	-	D	9.1920	*	Finished steel traffic

‡ Details taken from *Merthyr Historian Vol.2*
* No dates available

internal works transport system was becoming increasingly urgent, and, as early as 1831, the company acquired its first locomotive. It was built by the Neath Abbey Iron Company and, in the words of James W. Lowe was: 'A unique locomotive... consisting of 2 four-coupled units with a jack shaft between them driven by a pair of inclined outside cylinders. On the jack shaft was a gearwheel which meshed with the adjacent coupled axles on which were gearwheels. Two chimneys were fitted, one for each cylinder, and could be lowered to a horizontal position for passing through a tunnel'.

This highly unusual locomotive was followed by eight more from the same maker, delivery being spread over the period from 1832 to 1838. Initially, the earlier locomotives conformed to the Dowlais Works' plateway gauge of 4' 2", but in 1838 the system was reconstructed to the standard railway gauge of 4' 8½". The early Neath Abbey-built locomotives were regauged accordingly, and an 0-6-0 tender locomotive which had been ordered earlier in 1838 for the 4' 2" gauge was actually delivered as a standard gauge machine.

Over the whole period of iron and steel production at the Dowlais Works (1759-1930), approximately seventy different locomotives were used by the company at various times. Five of these, incidentally, were built to the 3ft gauge for use on the lines in the Bessemer steel making shop. The long list of locomotives embraced the products of many companies including such familiar names as Manning Wardle, Neilson, Hudswell Clarke & Rogers, Kitson, Sharp Stewart, Peckett, Fletcher Jennings and Clyde Engineering. The Dowlais company also acquired pre-grouping locomotives second- or third-hand from 'main line' companies; among these were six from the Great Western Railway. However, the most intriguing second-hand acquisition was undoubtedly Dowlais No.32. This has been recorded, somewhat confusingly, as either an outside cylinder Crewe-built L&NWR 2-4-0T or inside cylinder North London Railway 4-4-0T No.101, a product of Bow works in 1868! A photograph was published in *Illustrated Views of Merthyr and District, Vol2* purporting to

The immaculately turned-out Dowlais-built 0-4-0T No.42 QUEEN MARY, its nameplate bearing the words 'GRACIOUSLY NAMED BY HER MAJESTY IN PERSON... DURING HER VISIT TO DOWLAIS JUNE 27th 1912'. Four similar 'D' class locomotives were built at Dowlais between 1907 and 1920; their hefty proportions on a small wheelbase made them seem somewhat hunched, with an impression of considerable power. PHOTOGRAPH: DAVID THOMAS

The other Dowlais-built locomotive to be named during the Royal visit in June 1912 was No.40, which became KING GEORGE V. In its own way, it was every bit as smart as its rather more famous GWR namesake. PHOTOGRAPH: DAVID THOMAS

show No.32 at Dowlais, but the locomotive was still wearing its NLR 'No.101', and so there is no firm proof that No.101 and Dowlais No.32 were the same engine. (*If any reader has further information regarding the origins of Dowlais No.32, we would be interested to hear* - Ed).

Although the Dowlais company had undertaken minor repair work to its locomotives from the earliest days, it was not until 1901 that the firm decided to undertake its own major repairs, rebuilds and, more significantly, the actual construction of its own locomotives. Thus the scene was set for the construction of the true 'Dowlais Giants'.

The adoption of a 'new build' policy led to the appointment of George Robson as the Dowlais company's Locomotive Superintendent. Robson's background was essentially 'main line', as he had been an employee of the Taff Vale and Great Western companies. It is not altogether surprising, therefore, that the locomotives he designed at Dowlais had the appearance of thoroughbreds rather than the minimalist workhorses often associated with industrial railway systems.

The first tentative step by Robson was the major rebuild in 1903 of Dowlais No.27, a Husdwell Clarke 0-4-0ST of 1890. The next and more significant step was taken in January 1906 with the construction of a completely new locomotive, an 0-6-0T with 18" x 26" inside cylinders; it was allotted No.38 and was named ARTHUR KEEN after one of the Dowlais company's directors. In keeping with 'main line' practice - and clearly with an eye to further additions to the fleet - the locomotive was designated 'A' class.

The next locomotive built at Dowlais proved to be a more traditional style of engine. As Dowlais No.39, it was an out-side cylinder 0-4-0ST, designated 'C1' class; it emerged from the workshops in February 1907.

The year 1907 also witnessed the debut of locomotive No.40, an inside cylinder 0-4-0T of very substantial proportions. Weighing 35 tons, its boiler was pressed to the surprisingly high figure of 200lbs and was matched with a Belpaire firebox; at the time, this type of firebox was still an unusual feature in British 'main line' practice, and so its application to a humble industrial 0-4-0T was indeed a remarkable innovation. Yet again, one suspects that these features were a result of Robson's main line upbringing and, perhaps, his main line aspirations. No.40 was designated 'D' class, and there were eventually five examples of this type. To commemorate a Royal visit to Dowlais works on 27 June 1912, No.40 was named KING GEORGE V and its sister locomotive, No.42, was named QUEEN MARY.

The combination of a large boiler with a Belpaire firebox, together with small driving wheels of 3' 6" diameter, tended to give the 'D' class engines a massiveness of proportion which belied their true size. With cylinders of 14" diameter by 18" stroke, they produced a tractive effort of 14,280lb.

In 1908, a true giant of the industrial locomotive world emerged from the workshops at Dowlais. This was No.41 SANDYFORD, an 0-6-0T with 19" x 26" cylinders, driving wheels of 4' 0" and, like the 'D' class engines, a large boiler with a Belpaire firebox. The boiler was originally pressed to 200lb, which gave a remarkable tractive effort of 33,242lb - the pressure was later reduced to 180lb, but this still gave a highly respectable tractive effort of 30,772lb. In 1914, No.38 ARTHUR KEEN (the 0-6-0T of 1906) had its round-top fire-box replaced by a Belpaire, thus bringing it more into line with SANDYFORD.

SANDYFORD was built to transport materials from the Upper works at Dowlais to the Lower Works, the nearest gesture the company could make to possessing a main line. The locomotive's nearest claim to a main line passenger duty was during the Royal visit of 1912 when, having swapped nameplates with ARTHUR KEEN, it conveyed the Royal party around the works system in main line coaching stock which had been borrowed for the occasion.

The last new locomotive type to be conceived and constructed at Dowlais was seen in 1917. This was an outside cylinder 0-4-0T built for the 3' 0" gauge lines at the Bessemer steel plant where it was required to take bogies of cast iron ingot moulds to the ingot stripper. Only one locomotive of this new type was built at Dowlais - this was No.45, designated the 'H' class. Like its standard gauge counterparts its boiler was pressed to 200lbs, a very high figure indeed for an engine built to the dimensional constraints of the narrow gauge.

The final locomotive to be built at Dowlais was the fifth member of the 'D' class, which was completed in 1920. There was, however, another important chapter still to be seen - this unfolded in 1927 when 'D' class 0-4-0T No.44 PANT was rebuilt as an 0-6-0T. Precise dimensions of this locomotive in its rebuilt form have not come to light, but the end result can be seen in the accompanying photograph.

The Dowlais-built standard gauge locomotives were turned out in a livery which was usually described as medium green, lined out in yellow and black.

Unfortunately, these Dowlais locomotives were not destined to enjoy long lives.

No.42 with the Royal Coat of Arms, waiting to being named QUEEN MARY.
PHOTOGRAPH: JOHN RYAN

Economic circumstances and the concentration of steel making at the company's Cardiff and Margam plants in 1930 was effectively a death sentence for these fine machines. The lack of standard spare parts must also have contributed to their early demise. Only one of the Dowlais-built locomotives was transferred away from its birthplace for further duties. This was No.39, built in February 1907 and the only outside cylinder standard gauge side tank engine among the nine home-built examples. No.39 was transferred to Cardiff, becoming No.5, and following a period at Margam, was withdrawn from Cardiff East Moors in 1950, the last of the 'Dowlais Giants'.

An interesting postscript to this story is that Hornby has recently introduced models of both KING GEORGE V and QUEEN MARY. The type currently appears in the Hornby catalogue as numbers R2058 and R153, but they are shown in spurious liveries. Nevertheless, the very fact that the type lives on, albeit in miniature, is a fitting tribute to these fine locomotives.

Acknowledgements: During the preparation of this article, the following publications were consulted: Merthyr Historian Vol.1 *(articles by J.Owen, J.Gorss, R.Barnes and V.L.Winding), published by the Merthyr Tydfil Historical Society;* British Steam Locomotive Builders *by James Lowe;* Industrial Locomotives of South Wales and Monmouthshire *(Birmingham Loco Club Pocket Book No.6, 1951).*

As mentioned in the text, in 1927 'D' class 0-4-0T No.44 PANT was rebuilt as an 0-6-0T. We suspect that this picture was taken after the locomotive had been laid aside - it is in an abysmal condition, devoid of buffers and with the glass removed from the cab spectacles. **PHOTOGRAPH: DAVID THOMAS**

TREE AND LEAF
the Isle of Wight

To help ease the passage through the winter (although, of course, this *Annual* should really be enough on its own), we offer a reminder of what Britain *can* look like when the summer weather chooses to behave. Indeed, with a rather unseasonable 'summer holiday' feel, we take a brief look at the heady combination of sunshine and steam. Where better than the Isle of Wight, where the oft-used phrase 'sylvan setting' might even have been first applied to a railway. Our upper photograph shows Ventnor, the terminus of the Isle of Wight Railway's line from Ryde. This was something of a classic, being perched in a hollow beneath the cliffs; furthermore, as the railway line dived into a very dark tunnel only a few yards beyond the end of the platforms, it seemed as if the terminus was a completely isolated entity. Many railway modellers, after a few pints of Old Horizontal, must have imagined a giant fiddle yard behind the tunnel portal, with hands descending from the heavens to manoeuvre the stock. In our photograph, the tunnel is out of view to the right, but the remarkable setting of the terminus is clearly seen. The date is 30 August 1965 - the penultimate year or ordinary steam operations on the Isle of Wight - and an O2 0-4-4T (probably No.16) waits at the station. There seems to be a reasonable amount of activity, and the goods sidings, although rather herbaceous, are clearly still in use. Today, the station site is an industrial estate.

Our lower photograph shows the famous Smallbrook Junction, where the Newport line (foreground) and the Ventnor line (behind) diverged. The signal box was operational only between May and September - during the rest of the year it was switched out as the double-track section between there and Ryde was worked as two independent single lines. A six-coach train from Ventnor passes the 'box, with O2 No.16 in charge. PHOTOGRAPHS: D.TREVOR ROWE (upper); J.A.C.KIRKE; BARRY HOPER COLLECTION (lower)

The now-preserved Isle of Wight No.24 CALBOURNE - one of the last two O2s active on the island - produces a fine head of steam, presumably on the section between Brading and Sandown. PHOTOGRAPH: J.A.C.KIRKE; BARRY HOPER COLLECTION

NORTH BIERLEY SEWAGE WORKS

by Adrian Booth

Moments after the contents of the skips have been emptied, see below, one of the workmen has climbed back into the cab of Hunslet diesel W/No.7195 in order to propel the empty skips back towards the press house. PHOTOGRAPH: ADRIAN BOOTH

At one time, it was commonplace for sewage treatment works to use a narrow gauge railway for sludge and waste disposal. However, from the 1960s onwards most major sewage works were redeveloped and new operating processes introduced; usually, the narrow gauge railways did not survive the reconstruction schemes. One of the exceptions was the narrow gauge railway at North Bierley

Sewage Works - it not only survived, but was modernised at the same time as the works.

The works

North Bierley Sewage Works is located at grid reference SE179277 in the village of Oakenshaw, immediately to the south of the city of Bradford, though when the works were built in 1880 the site was outside

the city boundary in the borough of Spenborough. The works were intended to deal with the sewage from a 3,532-acre area in the southern part of Bradford which had hitherto drained naturally to the Hunsworth Beck, a tributary of the River Calder. The works passed into ownership of Bradford Corporation in 1899 and some partial reconstruction took place in 1903, but it was 1934 before major extensions

North Bierley Sewage Works was the penultimate British sewage works to have a locomotive-worked narrow gauge railway. The system was brought into use in the 1930s and remained operational for over fifty years. As with others of its ilk, it was worked by primitive looking diesel locomotives and basic, functional skip wagons - these aspects are evident in our series of photographs which were taken on 22 May 1979. Here, full skips are being emptied on to the tip, two workmen using spades to scrape the last remnants of sludge from the corners of the rear skip. Note the boards fixed to the inside of the skip bodies in order to increase capacity. The lorry loading point is in the foreground; skips were tipped to the left and the pressed sludge fell through the hole into the lorry waiting below. PHOTOGRAPH: ADRIAN BOOTH

Near the press house, the Hunslet diesel pushes the skips past the diesel fuel tank. PHOTOGRAPH: ADRIAN BOOTH

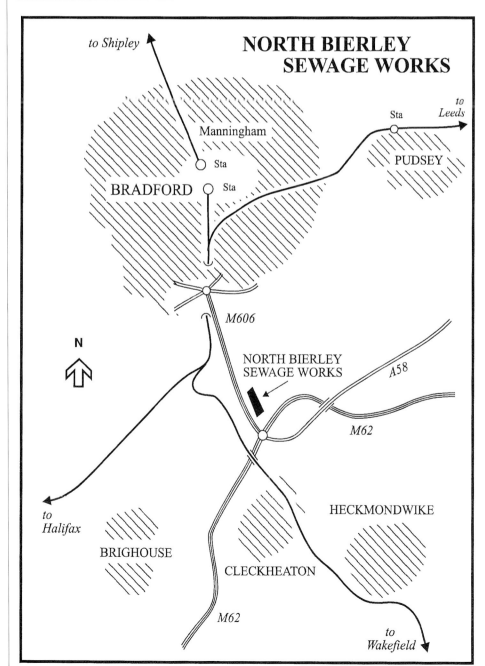

NORTH BIERLEY SEWAGE WORKS

to Shipley

Manningham

Sta

to Leeds

Sta

PUDSEY

BRADFORD

Sta

M606

N

NORTH BIERLEY SEWAGE WORKS

A58

M62

to Halifax

HECKMONDWIKE

BRIGHOUSE

CLECKHEATON

M62

to Wakefield

were put in hand. These took a couple of years to complete and were formally opened on 7 October 1936; they set the pattern of operation for the next thirty years.

By the mid-1930s, the works served a population of about 32,000 in southern Bradford, although the volume of sewage increased as new residential and industrial expansion took place in the area. The sewage was stated then to be of 'average' strength, with a considerable contribution from textile, chemical and metal finishing industries. The treatment processes followed orthodox lines, of sedimentation followed by biological filtration; there were no special problems, unlike other sites such as Esholt Works (featured in BYLINES 1:3) which had to deal with effluent created by the wool scouring industry. By May 1979 North Bierley Works served a population of 40,000 and still serviced a couple of chemical firms.

When the sewage arrived at North Bierley Works it was initially directed into two detritus tanks - used alternately - and then through a ten-inch main to a pneumatically operated sludge ram, from which it was discharged to sludge storage tanks. The sludge leaving the tanks was recorded as it passed to a bank of six sedimentation tanks - each measuring 50ft wide by 90ft long and 6ft deep - which had a combined capacity of 1,012,500 gallons. The sludge was then sent to an electrically-operated pumping plant, from where it was delivered to the storage tank. The effluent from the sludge storage tank flowed to the biological filter beds (which had been constructed in 1936); these were two acres in extent, 5ft 6in deep, with a bed of hard coal graded one to two inches providing the filter medium. After passing through humus tanks, the treated effluent flowed through a 27-inch pipe and was dis-

A view of the modern press house, showing the three parallel 2ft 0in gauge roads leading inside. Skips are visible on the right and centre roads. The track in the foreground is conspicuously well ballasted. PHOTOGRAPH: ADRIAN BOOTH

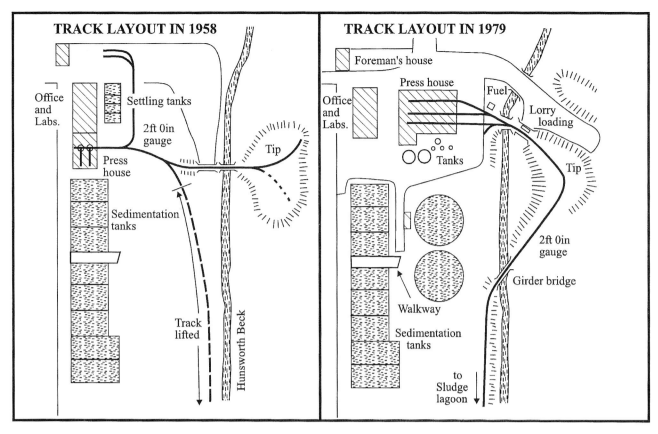

TRACK LAYOUT IN 1958

Office and Labs.

Settling tanks

2ft 0in gauge

Tip

Press house

Sedimentation tanks

Track lifted

Hunsworth Beck

TRACK LAYOUT IN 1979

Foreman's house

Press house

Fuel

Office and Labs.

Lorry loading

Tanks

Tip

2ft 0in gauge

Girder bridge

Walkway

Sedimentation tanks

to Sludge lagoon

charged over a weir into Hunsworth Beck. In a typical year - 1964 - a total of some 19,500 tons of sludge was collected in the detritus tanks, sedimentation tanks and storm tanks. The sludge was lifted by ram to three filter presses - of a type similar to those used at Esholt - where it was treated with lime and pressed for about three hours into 'cake' form. Much of the 'cake' was disposed of to local farmers. The detritus waste was taken away be means of a narrow gauge railway to be deposited on a tip adjacent to the works. The filter press house was a low, cramped, building with short loading sidings reached by a pair of turntables, and so each wagon had to be laboriously manhandled into position.

The works had to deal with an ever increasing amount of sewage, and so, in the late 1960s further extensions to the works - and modernisation of the existing facilities - were undertaken. The improvements to the works increased the capacity of the site, and the treatment process was aided by the addition of effluent recirculation.

The narrow gauge railway

The internal railway at North Bierley Sewage Works was constructed to a gauge of 2ft 0in. As far as can be determined, the railway was constructed while the extension work was being undertaken in 1934-36. The first locomotive arrived at North Bierley in 1935, while the extension of the works was underway. The locomotive was ordered by the City of Bradford Sewage Department from Motor Rail Ltd of Bedford; it was one of the maker's standard four-wheel machines (W/No.5458), weigh-

ing a mere 2½ tons and fitted with a Dorman 'Type 4MRX' petrol engine which had a variable power output from 20-35hp. It was delivered to North Bierley Works on 11 July 1935, and for the next eighteen years had sole charge of the traffic. Its duties involved taking full skips from the filter press house, either to the loading dock (if the 'cake' had been sold), or to a tip at the remote southern end of the works.

The Motor Rail locomotive was transferred to Esholt Works in 1953, being replaced at North Bierley by another newly-built four-wheel petrol locomotive, this time one of F.C.Hibberd & Co's 'Planet' locomotives, W/No.3627. The new arrival had the luxury of a cab, but otherwise adhered to the manufacturer's traditional design.

There was another change of motive power at North Bierley in September 1961 when the 'Planet' was sent to Esholt Works for storage; it was later acquired by Bradford Industrial Museum for preservation. (It is now at Amberley Museum). The 'Planet' was replaced at North Bierley by another Motor Rail - this was W/No.8959, another 2½-ton machine generally similar to the previous one, but with plate frames and a Dorman 20/28hp 'Type 2DWD' diesel engine, with final drive to the axles by roller chains. It had been built in 1944 for the Ship Canal Sand Company who had a 1ft 9in gauge system at their Mount Vernon Sand Quarries at Weaste near Salford. It later passed to Messrs.Crowley, Russell & Co, a firm of contractors, who

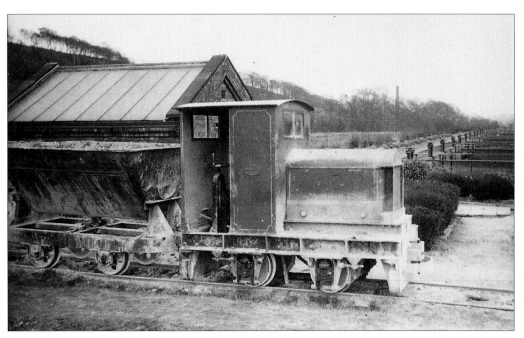

North Bierley's second locomotive was petrol-engined 'Planet', W/No.3627. It was photographed in action on 13 April 1958, hauling a rake of the original Hudson side-tipping skips. PHOTOGRAPH: MIKE SWIFT

sold it to the City of Bradford Sewage Department in 1961. It initially went to the workshops at Esholt Works where it was regauged to 2ft 0in, and was later sent to North Bierley, where it remained in sole charge of duties until 1974.

The 1970s

As mentioned earlier, a programme of major improvements to North Bierley Works commenced in the late 1960s. These became fully operational in 1974. A major part of the modernisation involved the replacement of the old, cramped, filter press house by a new, tall, spacious building with a concrete floor. The new filter press house had three parallel tracks set into the floor; the tracks emerged on to a paved apron in front of the doorway and then joined together to cross Hunsworth Beck by means of a bridge to reach the sludge tip. At one time there had been a line on the west side of the beck to a remote tip and sludge lagoon, but that line was derelict and partly lifted by the 1950s. However, much of the abandoned section was reinstated during the improvement works of the late 1960s/early 1970s - in the main, portable track with steel sleepers was used, though some timber sleepers were installed where the formation was soft. The reinstatement of the line required the construction of a substantial girder bridge across the beck.

The old Motor Rail locomotive (W/No.5458) returned to North Bierley Works *circa* 1972, but only to be stored; it remained for a year or so before going back to Esholt where it was scrapped *circa* 1975. There was, however a permanent new arrival at North Bierley in the 1970s. In 1974 a new locomotive was acquired to work on the newly laid railway system. This was Hunslet Engine Co W/No.7195, a four-wheel diesel-mechanical which was fitted with a two-speed gearbox and powered by a four-cylinder Perkins 'Type 4.203' engine developing 39hp; it was noteworthy, being the very last 39hp example to be manufactured - locomotives of this type were subsequently fitted with 50hp, and later still, 52hp, engines. The new North Bierley Hunslet was painted dark green with black and yellow chevrons on the buffer beams; it had a pillar cab, from the rear of which hung a bell.

When the new filter press house was installed at North Bierley, new and much larger skips were supplied (these were specially designed to suit the new press house) by Firth Brothers of Scissett, near Huddersfield. The new skips replaced a half-dozen or so Hudson-built side-tipping skips, which were transferred to Esholt Works. The new skips were subsequently modified by the addition of wooden boards - affixed to the inside faces of the skip bodies - to increase capacity. Safety chains were also fitted to avoid over-tipping and pos-

sible derailment. In 1979 there were also three spare skip frames strewn around the site, plus a very heavy skip with 'Spoorijzer Delft' on its axleboxes.

In 1979 - when most of the accompanying photographs were taken - the narrow gauge railway was in use five days a week, the operations being relatively simple. Three trains, each of four skips, were positioned inside the filter press house by the Hunslet diesel. Chutes were positioned in the roof above the skips to enable filter cake to be dropped and, when all skips in a rake were filled, they were pulled outside. They were then hauled to the unloading bay - where the skip contents were discharged into a lorry below - or a little further along the line to a tip. The empty wagons were then returned to the press house and the process repeated with the next full set. The track to the far end of the works was overgrown in places, and apparently had been disused for some time. Indeed, one wondered why it had been reinstated at all during the redevelopments. The spare Motor Rail locomotive (W/No.8959) was dumped on this track, some distance from the works, and was beginning to look somewhat neglected.

The narrow gauge operation at North Bierley continued into the late 1980s, its remarkable survival undoubtedly due to the newly installed and purpose-built rail-orientated plant. In its latter days the narrow gauge system was a major rarity, with practically all other British sewage works railways having long since been replaced by other methods such as road transport. The railway was still in use when visited by the author on 20 February 1985. It worked from 8.30am to 3.45pm. The track had been severed just beyond the unloading point, although the long track beyond that point was still in situ, albeit rusted and badly overgrown. Apparently, six of the large skips were badly in need of replacement but, because of their

large non-standard specification, replacements were difficult to find. Nevertheless, the railway soldiered on for a while, but no solution was found to the problem of replacing the life-expired skips and so, before too long, the railway was abandoned in favour of road transport. North Bierley Sewage Works was the penultimate British sewage site to be locomotive-worked - the very last, incidentally, was the Severn Trent Water Authority's works at Stoke Bardolph near Nottingham.

At North Bierley, the very last of the track and skips were taken from the site in January 1997. Today, liquid sludge is taken from the sewage works by road tanker to an incinerator in the Calder Valley. Of the last two locomotives at North Bierley, the spare Motor Rail (W/No 8959) was sent to the Yorkshire Water Authority - successors to the City of Bradford Sewage Department - Bradford depot in 1982. It is believed to have been sold to British Car Auctions in 1984, although all trace of it has been lost. Perhaps a reader can enlighten us if it still exists? As for the modern Hunslet (W/No.7195), it was sold to the Festiniog Railway and moved there in March 1993. When inspected by the author at the Festiniog's Boston Lodge Works on 10 September 1996, it had been repainted in light blue livery. It still carried its thin brass worksplate, and had the name HAROLD applied.

Author's note: I wish to thank Mick Burgoyne, Bob Darvill, Mike Swift, and Don Townsley for their help, and also Ms.Caroline Atkins of the Yorkshire Water Authority.

Editor's note: An article about North Bierley Sewage Works by Adrian Booth appeared in Issue No.09 of The Narrow Gauge *(the journal of the Narrow Gauge Railway Society). With permission of the NGRS, it has been updated and considerably expanded by its original author for use here.*

Is it a bird? Is it a plane? No - it is, in fact, Motor Rail diesel locomotive W/No.8959, which was dumped out of use along the lengthy line which ran southerly from the sewage works to a former tip. Its livery - if one can call it such - is green and grey. PHOTOGRAPH: ADRIAN BOOTH

On The Beach - Felixstowe Beach station, 27 May 1965

There were few places on the Great Eastern (a railway which after all, famously derived its living from root vegetables) where the seaside holiday habit was afforded any particularly lavish degree of accommodation. Felixstowe was no exception. The town had a complicated little history, with a sort of private railway and its own locomotives operating briefly until the GER took hold in the 1870s. From the late 1890s trains reversed at the new Town station (where there was a turntable) and ran through Beach station, shown here from the outside in all its clapboard glory, and from the crossing at the country end to terminate at Pier station. In the distance, on a site obscured by the coal wagons (lower photograph), there was once even a two-road engine shed and three-road carriage shed. These 'faded away' in the best GE tradition and engines used the turntable and siding at Town station. BOTH PHOTOGRAPHS: DEREK CLAYTON

THE LMS SENTINELS
An unconsummated flirtation

by Bill Aves

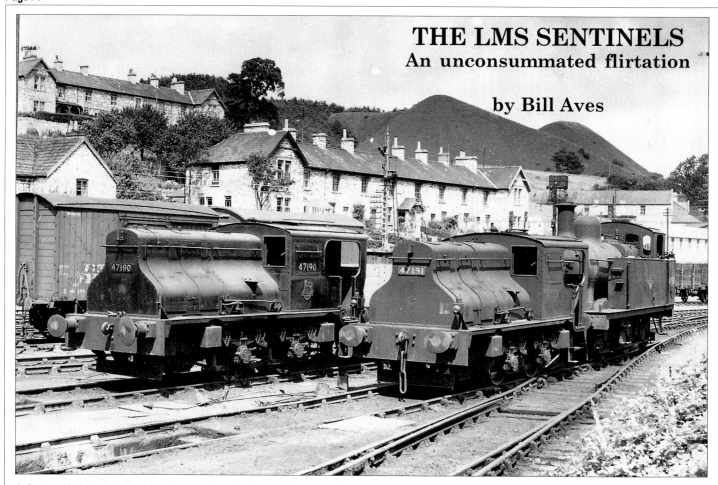

A Sentinel double take? Well, not quite... The two Somerset & Dorset Sentinels eventually became BR Nos.47190 and 47191, and were photographed together outside Radstock shed on 22 July 1958. The S&D line is behind the shed yard (adjacent to the raised signal) and the spoil tips of Tyning Colliery and the houses in Waldegrave Terrace (above) and Waterloo Road (below) provide the backdrop. As can be seen, the two S&D Sentinels weren't absolutely identical. The positioning of the BR numbers on the cab side and the front differs on each locomotive, and only one of the pair sports a BR crest. Furthermore, No.47190 has odd-size round buffers (one of which looks decidedly askew!) and no front couplings, while No.47191 has oval buffers and a chain coupling. The Jinty at the rear is No 47557. A classic 'S&D at Radstock' scene... PHOTOGRAPH: R.C.RILEY

The LNER's use of Sentinel shunting locomotives and railcars has been fairly well chronicled, not least in our sister publication, *British Railways Illustrated* (Vol.3 Nos.10 and 12), but it is less well known and certainly less well documented is that the LMS also experimented with Sentinel designs and purchased railcars and shunting locomotives for normal service. In all, no less than sixteen different Sentinel types ran on, or were ordered by, the LMS and its subsidiaries. It is apparent, even from the incomplete evidence which survives, that the company seems not to have carried through its early interest in the Sentinels, making inadequate preparation for both the employment and maintenance of the new machines. As a result, inevitable teething troubles were not resolved, while re-design and development were never pursued. This was no doubt partly because of the small number of railcars (15) and shunters (8, including 2 from the Somerset & Dorset) which the LMS actually took into stock. It was also symptomatic of the malaise which affected the Company's locomotive policy in the first ten years after the 1923 Grouping.

The Sentinel Waggon Works Ltd was established in 1918 with the renaming of the Glasgow firm of Alley & MacLellan following their move to new premises in Shrewsbury three years earlier. The firm was already prominent in the manufacture of steam road wagons when they published their catalogue of steam rail vehicles and 'Super-Sentinel' engines in 1922 and, although no railway vehicles were built to these particular designs, considerable interest was aroused in railway circles, where competition from motor buses was becoming a substantial threat. In June 1923 the company built its first railcar for the 3ft 6in gauge Jersey Railways and Tramways, and in 1924 exhibited another at the British Empire Exhibition at Wembley. In these railcars, the power unit was articulated to the saloon and comprised a vertical boiler with a twin cylinder, double-acting horizontal engine using chain drive. The coachwork was built by Cammell Laird & Co of Nottingham; this firm became part of the Metropolitan-Cammell group in 1929, and continued to construct railcars there until the factory was closed in 1931.

The early trials

The mainline companies were attracted by the potential of Sentinel's economical, lightweight, inexpensive machines, and in August/September 1924 the LNER tried out two railcars, similar in design to the Jersey car, differing from each other only in the size of their boilers. These were Sentinel Works Nos.5654 and 5657, the latter with the larger boiler. The trials showed promise and the LNER bought both cars in May 1925 (W/No.5654 having been rebuilt with the larger type of power plant), becoming Nos 13E and 12E respectively.

The LMS was not far behind, and undertook trials with a similar car, Works No.5655, on the Ripley branch, working from Derby, in March 1925 (passenger services between Derby and Ripley were withdrawn on 1 June 1930). Contrary to some accounts, this railcar did not become LMS No.2233 (see below), but was returned to the makers who loaned it to the LNER for

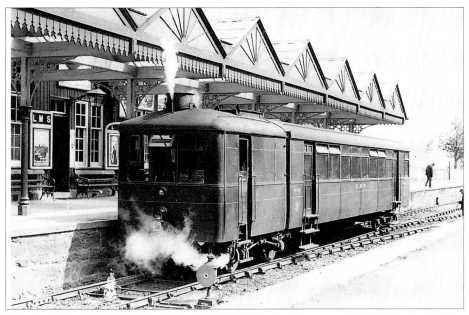

As related in the text, most of the LMS's Sentinel railcars worked in Scotland. One of the Scottish contingent was No.4149 (later renumbered 29907 in carriage stock), which was photographed at Strathpeffer on 18 May 1928. PHOTOGRAPH: H.C.CASSERLEY

a few months, and by early September (if not before) was sold to Leys Malleable Castings of Derby. The LMS's interest in Sentinel shunting locomotives was therefore manifest a few months before the LNER conducted its first dynamometer tests with the Derwent Valley Light Railway's engine, W/No.6076, in May 1925. (It is also of interest that the third of the small Sentinel shunters which had been built for stock - W/No.5735 - was purchased by Samuel Williams & Sons of Dagenham Dock - see *Railway Bylines* Vol.2 No.6).

The LMS(NCC) purchase

While Sentinel railcars and shunters were still going through their paces on the mainland, the Northern Counties Committee (the LMS's subsidiary in Northern Ireland) had gone ahead and bought one of each, W/No.5750 (the railcar) and W/No.5751 (the shunter). The railcar was taken into stock as No.401 in the NCC Coaching Stock List in April 1925, and the shunter as No.91 in the Locomotive List the next month. They had similar chain-driven power units which had two cylinders of 6¾" x 9", a boiler pressed to 275lbs and measuring 2' 8" in diameter and 4' 4" in height. Those dimensions were very similar to those of the two cars bought by the LNER in May 1925.

The NCC's railcar and shunter were clearly standard Sentinel products of the period, but despite the very early interest shown in Ulster, no further acquisitions followed. The railcar and shunter both had very brief working lives, being withdrawn in 1932.

Series orders

Sentinel wrote to Mr.J.H.Follows, the LMS's General Superintendent at Derby, in July 1925 enclosing catalogues of their locomotives and the Sentinel-Cammell railcars. As a result, Colonel Rudgard, the

more trials in the Newcastle area in September 1926, before eventually selling it to the standard-gauge Jersey Eastern Railway in 1927. When the Jersey Eastern closed two years later, it was bought by Jersey Railways & Tramways and re-gauged to 3ft 6in by them.

It is clear that the trials on the Ripley branch were encouraging and another chain-driven, articulated railcar, W/No.6177, was the subject of further proving by the LMS. The building date of this car (in which the driving-end configuration differed slightly from the original trial railcar, W/No.5655) is uncertain, but it was probably ordered in the second half of 1925 and sent for trials on the LMS early in 1926.

Meanwhile, the LMS had tried out a small Sentinel shunter. This was W/No.5733, one of three which are believed to have been ordered for stock in late 1924, each incorporating minor differences. W/No.5733 weighed 15 tons and had the 7ft wheelbase which was common to most of the type. It was loaned to the LMS - it is known to have arrived at Crewe by January 1925 - and was used at Crewe Works where Major Hewitt Beames (this was H.P.M.Beames, the former L&NWR Locomotive Superintendent who, after the grouping, had been controversially demoted and placed in charge of the LMS Western Division) took a keen interest in the novel machine. However, the locomotive was returned to Shrewsbury after only

A splendid portrait of LMS Sentinel railcar No.4146 at Ayr, *circa* 1931/32. The seal between engine portion and the coach portion is clearly visible. Note the lack of conventional drawgear or buffing gear - the absence of the former was simply because the railcars were not intended to haul or be hauled, while the absence of the latter was a well intentioned aid to weight reduction. However, these weight-saving features proved to be a handicap when 'dead' railcars required moving at the sheds, movement having to be undertaken, instead, by means of the towing hooks (seen under the lower lamp). Another point of interest is the partly open coal shute doors on the roof behind the driving compartment. PHOTOGRAPH: BARRY HOPER COLLECTION

The LMS's subsidiary in Northern Ireland - the Northern Counties Committee - purchased one locomotive and one railcar from the Sentinel company in 1925. They were, of course, built to the NCC's gauge of 5ft 3in. The locomotive became NCC No.91; unlike its counterparts in England and Scotland it had a wheelbase of 8ft 6in - its greater length, with the larger cab with two side windows, are very evident. Although No.91 generated considerable interest, no other Sentinels were ordered by the NCC; furthermore, No.91 lasted in service only until 1932. This picture was taken at the NCC depot in Belfast on 5 August 1930. PHOTOGRAPH: H.C.CASSERLEY

Assistant Motive Power Superintendent, visited Norwich on 26 August with a party of LNER officials to 'inspect the working of LNER car No.12E' which had been in use in that area for three months. Rudgard was impressed, and recommended that '...this coach should be adopted where possible' - this recommendation was based on evidence that the railcar could save an estimated 750 tons of coal per annum, saved one man on every shift, and had already brought about increased revenue on the routes on which it had been employed. Rudgard also considered that it would be advisable to seek the views of Mr.Pepper of the Northern Counties Committee regarding their railcar (W/No.5750) which had, by this time, been in service for four months.

Colonel Rudgard's report, combined with the LMS's experience with the railcars they had tried out, was sufficient for the Locomotive Committee to approve, on 28 July 1926, the purchase of thirteen cars from the Sentinel company, under LMS Lot 40. These comprised the 'prototype', W/ No.6177, which was taken into stock as No.2233 (in series with the former Midland steam railcars in the Coaching Stock List) and an order for twelve generally similar units which was placed with Sentinel on 18 October. These were delivered as W/Nos.6777-6788 in June and July 1927; they were 44-seat articulated, lightweight cars without normal buffers or drawgear, with vertical engines and chain-drive, and had 2' 6" diameter wheels (as fitted to most Sentinel shunting locomotives). Like the LNER prototypes, the LMS railcars were 56' 5" over their bodies, although the LNER's examples were always quoted as seating 52 passengers, including the tip-up seats installed in the luggage compartment. The new LMS cars were given Coaching Stock Nos.4143-4154, but not in the order of their works numbers

(see Table Two); they were covered by Coaching Stock Diagram D1779. Photographs reveal that LMS Nos.4143-4154 incorporated a number of detail differences in bodywork and the configuration of doors and windows from the prototype railcar, LMS No.2233. Another difference was that No.2233, like the LNER prototype cars, had the earlier type of outside-framed non-driving bogie.

Three of the new cars (LMS Nos.4145, 4147 and 4148) were given larger boilers in May 1929, and as late as June 1931 the Locomotive Committee recommended similar modifications to three more. Three '25LTS' boilers (this was Sentinel's abbreviation for '25% Larger Than Standard' boilers) were the subject of a spares order for 'LMS St.Rollox' dated 14 September 1931, and it is assumed that these boilers were supplied and duly fitted to three other railcars. In the 1933 Coaching Stock renumbering, LMS Nos.2233 and 4143-4154 became Nos.29900-29912. The operational history of these thirteen railcars is set out separately - suffice it to say that most of them were initially used on branch lines in the LMS's Northern Division (i.e. Scotland).

The LMS's Sentinel railcars lasted for less than ten years. All except No.29910 were withdrawn in 1935, the Locomotive Committee having concluded in April of that year that: '...the vehicles are now out of date from a passenger carrying point of view and compare unfavourably with more recent developments in rail coaches and with modern road vehicles. It is not considered practicable to re-design or alter them to a satisfactory standard to meet present day requirements... vehicle No.29910 (which, presumably, had been one of the three cars to have received a larger boiler as a consequence of the Locomotive Committee recommendation of June 1931) to be retained for service on a branch line in Scotland

where the question or road competition does not arise'.

...and locomotives

The Sentinel shunting locomotives appeared to offer important advantages: a low overall weight and maximum axle load (about 20 tons and 10 tons respectively), a very short wheelbase (7ft), suitability for one-man operation, and low coal consumption. Few existing classes could compete, and an 'off the peg' buy would obviate the need for an in-house design.

With these proclaimed advantages in mind, the LMS obtained a Sentinel shunter for trials; this was W/No.6735, built to the makers standard design in November 1926 - this was, of course, seven or eight months before the LMS took delivery of its railcars. (After its trials with the LMS at Newton Heath were over, W/ No.6735 was returned to the makers; in 1928 it went on trial to the LNER, who purchased it the following year). During its period on trial with the LMS, W/ No.6735 apparently gave reasonable satisfaction, but there must have been some lingering doubts as to the locomotive's capabilities as a more powerful Sentinel shunter was obtained later for further trials. This was W/No.6515, which had already had an interesting history: built for the GWR in August 1926 (becoming GWR No.12), it was fitted with vacuum brakes and steam heating for passenger work and was tried on the Malmesbury branch and at Fowey, but proved unsatisfactory and was taken out of stock and returned to the makers in January 1927. Sentinel then fitted it with a 25LTS boiler; in this form, it underwent passenger train trials on the Shropshire & Montgomeryshire Railway, and in October 1927 was again tried by the GWR on the Malmesbury branch. In April 1929 the makers loaned it to the LMS, who put it to work in the Shropshire

Union Yard at Shrewsbury. After trials, it returned once again to Sentinel who used it as their works shunter at Shrewsbury. It was sold in October 1934 to Messrs. T.E.Grey at Burton Latimer, becoming their No.2, named ISEBROOK. Somewhat fittingly for a locomotive with such a chequered history, it is now preserved and can be seen at Quainton Road.

The LMS's trials with W/No.6515 were encouraging enough for the Locomotive Committee to approve the placing of an order, on 23 October 1929, with Sentinel's for four standard two-speed shunters with the larger boiler. The order was placed as Lot 65. However, even this order was not the end of the trials process, as the Locomotive Committee's report to the Board reveals: '...*preliminary tests which have been carried out with a 100 hp "Sentinel" shunting engine indicate the possibility of appreciable savings being effected by the employment of these engines in lieu of shunting tank engines in goods yards and to enable further experiments to be made, it was recommended that authority be given for the purchase of four "Sentinel" shunting locomotives at a total cost of £6,180...*'.

The four engines, W/Nos.8209-8212, were delivered to the LMS at Shrewsbury shed during July 1930, as LMS Nos.7160-7163. They were two-speed engines, similar to LNER Class Y3, of which the first had been completed as W/No.7140 as long ago as December 1927, but were 6" longer over their buffers (19' 4" instead of 18' 10"). Their principal dimensions are given in the accompanying table.

They were renumbered as Nos.7180-7183 in 1939, as part of the process of clearing parts of the 7XXX number series for new diesel shunters. After working in various parts of the system for a dozen or so years, from the early 1940s Nos.7180, 7181, 7183 spent their time at Sutton Oak or singly at Shrewsbury for the Clee Hill quarries (*see RAILWAY BYLINES* Vol.1, No.2). The fourth engine, LMS No.7182, was shedded at Ayr throughout its twenty-six years service. The four locomotives were withdrawn between July 1953 and November 1956, and thus enjoyed a very similar working lifespan to the much larger number of Sentinel shunters employed by the LNER; nevertheless the 'further experiments' contemplated by the LMS in October 1929 did not lead them to purchase additional similar engines.

There were other orders for Sentinel shunting locomotives during the 1920s. The Somerset and Dorset Joint Railway took delivery of two new Sentinel shunters, W/Nos.7587 and 7588, in February and May 1929 respectively, to replace the antiquated saddle tanks, known as the 'Dazzlers', which were used at Radstock. The S&D's Sentinels were larger than those purchased directly by the LMS, being of the double-engined 200hp type, with a two-cylinder vertical engine driving each axle. The first shunter of this type, incidentally, was W/No.7109, which had been ordered in 1927 by the Croydon Gas Company for their gas works at Waddon Marsh. Before delivery it had been sent to the LMS Carriage Works at Newton Heath for trials; it worked coal wagons to the boiler house and was also tested on a train of no less than fifteen bogie coaches and a 20-ton brake van.

As for the Somerset & Dorset's pair, the purchase had been approved by the S&D Joint Committee on July 1928, the locomotives being intended '...for use on the Ludlows, Writhlington and Clandown Branches...', but this told only part of the story. The Sentinels, with their low cab roofs and dropped footplates, were one of the very few locomotive types which could pass under the severely limited clearance of 'Marble Arch', the bridge which carried the tramway from Tyning Colliery across part of the S&D yard at Radstock. The two Sentinels became S&D Nos.101 and 102. When new, the first of the pair was evaluated on shunting duties at the works yard at Highbridge. One particular factor which impressed the management was that it consumed only about 8 or 9 cwt of coal per day, compared to the 20cwt of an ordinary shunting locomotive. After its trials at Highbridge, No.101 was duly moved to its intended home at Radstock where it was soon joined by No.102. When the LMS took over full responsibility for S&D locomotive matters in 1930, the two Sentinels became LMS Nos.7190 and 7191. This re-numbering, whether by accident or design, left a number block vacant for 25 or so new Sentinels!

One-offs - still more trials

At a meeting on 24 April 1929, the LMS Locomotive Committee approved the purchase of an additional railcar, under Lot 64; this railcar was described as: '...*an improved Sentinel-Cammell coach which has been on trial since 18 August 1928, and which has proved satisfactory for use on sections of the line where the gradient is heavy, be purchased at a cost of £3,850, for use in Scotland*'. Unlike the LMS's earlier railcars in which the engine portion was articulated to the saloon, this was a larger, heavier, rigid, 6-cylinder gear-driven machine with conventional buffers and drawgear. It bore Sentinel W/No.7362 and was, in fact, only the third rigid railcar built for service in the British Isles. (Sentinel's internal order dated 16 January 1928 referred to a '...*new type geared rail coach power unit...which will go on trial with the LMS*')

The new car became LMS No.4349 (No.29913 after the 1933 Coaching Stock re-numbering). Its precise activities in Scotland prior to its formal purchase by the LMS are unrecorded; however, when ex-

The bodywork of the NCC's Sentinel articulated railcar was fairly similar to that of the later LMS cars, though a separate saloon was provided for first class passengers, and it had a sliding window next to the door of the engine compartment, whereas the LMS cars had a blank panel. The railcar is seen standing alongside the NCC's Sentinel shunter at Belfast on 5 August 1930.

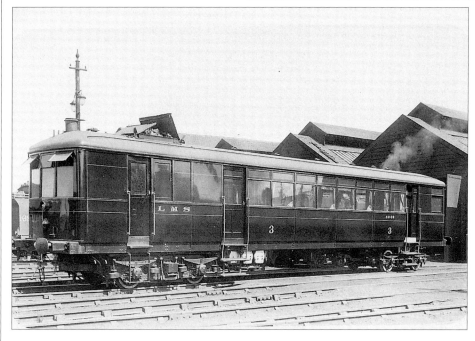

works from the Metro-Cammell factory at Nottingham, it is believed to have undergone at least some of its initial trials in and around Ambergate. No.4349 was covered by Coaching Stock Diagram D1842; its weight was quoted as 25 tons, and it had the 2ft 6in diameter wheels as fitted to the earlier LMS articulated cars. It had seating for 44, two by two (the saloons of the similar LNER cars were arranged to provide two by three seating, explaining their larger capacity). It seems to have spent its life in Scotland, until withdrawal in December 1939, having outlived the other LMS Sentinel railcars by more than two years.

The Isle of Axholme railcar

One other Sentinel railcar remains to be discussed. We need to go back to 1926, in which year the LMS tried out their prototype lightweight Sentinel railcar, No.2233, on the Isle of Axholme Joint Railway. This line extended for 19½ miles from Goole to Haxey & Epworth and was jointly owned by the LMS and LNER (prior to the grouping the parties had been the L&Y and NER); it was the LMS's responsibility to provide the motive power, and this was done from Goole shed. The trials of the prototype railcar on the Axholme line had clearly been promising, as in 1928 Sentinel began work on two 6-cylinder engines and a Woolnough 3-drum boiler for a: '200hp LMS trial car for the Isle of Axholme', the job being designated W/No.7565. However, the construction and delivery of W/No.7565 was not straightforward. In August 1928 the order was changed to 'LMS 200hp LMS trial car' - i.e. deleting the reference to the Isle of Axholme - and in April 1929 the components were reallocated to 'LNER Car W/No.7822'. This was eventually completed in June 1930 as the first LNER 200hp twin-engined railcar, No.2281 OLD JOHN BULL. Whether the LMS or the Isle of Axholme had ever been associated with this new, advanced design is uncertain, but it was an indirect prelude to the LMS's acquisition of an additional railcar.

The LMS placed an order, approved on 28 February 1930, under Lot 75, for a single car for the Isle of Axholme Joint Railway. This was a unique 64-seat, rigid, 6-cylinder railcar (i.e. similar to No.4349 and the LNER 'Diagram 97' cars, but 3ft longer). The additional seating capacity was presumably a reflection of experience gained during the earlier trials, but traffic estimates proved to be over-optimistic and, instead, passenger services were withdrawn from the Axholme line on 17 June 1933. The Axholme car (W/No.8228) had entered service as LMS No.44 in December 1930 but was in LNER green and cream livery. It was allotted LMS No.29987 in 1933, but was not actually renumbered; the LMS, having no further use for it, sold it to the LNER, who took it into stock as their No.51915 in November 1933. It was withdrawn in July 1944, having been used on local services around Wigan from 1934

Middle. The only LMS Sentinel shunter which definitely worked in Scotland was No.7162, which spent all of its life allocated to Ayr where it was known to crews as 'The Chipcart'. Becoming BR No.47182, it was withdrawn from Ayr in February 1956, being replaced there by ex-LNER Sentinel No.68138. PHOTOGRAPH: R.M.CASSERLEY COLLECTION

Bottom. Sporting a smart LMS livery - very probably having just been delivered - is No.7163. The Sentinel worksplate, complete with symbol, is evident. PHOTOGRAPH: F.W.SHUTTLEWORTH COLLECTION

Top. The LMS's gear-driven rigid Sentinel railcar was No.4349, later No.29913. It is seen at Hamilton shed, having been generously coaled, *circa* 1930/31. PHOTOGRAPH: T.J.EDGINGTON COLLECTION

The two Somerset & Dorset Sentinels were of a different type to any others ever used by a British 'main line' company. The first of the pair to be delivered was S&D No.101 (which later became LMS No.7190), seen here in unlined black livery at Radstock shed on 21 May 1929. This locomotive became the last LMS Sentinel to remain in service - it was withdrawn, as BR No.47190, in March 1961. PHOTOGRAPH: H.C.CASSERLEY

to 1940, thereafter leading a nomadic existence.

More locomotives

There were still two more shunters to come. In July 1931, the LMS's Locomotive Committee recommended: '...that a 100hp "Sentinel" Industrial type steam locomotive be purchased at an estimated cost of £1,315 for shunting purposes at Clee Hill Summit (LMS and GW Joint) in lieu of an 0-4-0 shunting tank engine... The LMS company are responsible for supplying the shunting power at this point and it is estimated that the carrying out of the proposal will effect a saving of £234 per annum in wages (the locomotive was intended for one-man operation), in addition to reduced fuel consumption'. It will be noted in the foregoing extract that the LMS referred to an 'industrial type' Sentinel locomotive. The manufacturers differentiated between 'railway' and 'industrial' types, in that the latter were of generally lighter construction, with plate frames instead of extensively braced channel frames, and were equipped to a more basic standard.

TABLE ONE: LMS Sentinel railcars - dimensions and details
(a) principal dimensions

Works No.	Type	Seats	Cylinders	Boiler pressure	Boiler size	Wheels	Total length	Weight full
5655	Articulated, chain drive; horizontal engine		(2) 6¾" x 9"			2' 6"		
5750	Articulated chain drive; vertical engine		(2) 6¾" x 9"	275lb	2' 8½" x 4' 4"	2' 6"		
6177	Articulated chain drive; vertical engine	44	(2) 6¾" x 9"	275lb	2' 8½" x 4' 4"	2' 6"		21t 0c
6777-88	Articulated chain drive; vertical engine	44	(2) 6¾" x 9"	275lb	2' 8½" x 4' 4"	2' 6"	58' 0"	21t 0c
7362	Rigid, gear drive	44	(6) 6" x 7"	300lb	3' 1" x 5' 1½"	2' 6"		25t 0c
7565	Double-engined	-	-	-	-	-	-	-
8228	Rigid, gear drive	64	(6) 6" x 7"	300lb	3' 1" x 5' 1½"	3' 1"	65' 8"	29t 5c
8817-19	Sentinel Doble oil-fired compound double-engined	-	-	-	-	-	-	-

(b) detail differentials (based largely on personal observation and photographic evidence)

	'Ripley' car	LMS coaching stock numbers No.29900	Nos.29901-12	No.29913	No.44 (Axholme)
Roof filler	No	No	Yes	Yes	Yes
Rain strips	Two *	Two §	Two *	Full-length	Full-length
Door handrails	Short	Short	Long	Long	Short
Footsteps	Two	Three small	Three large	Three large	Three small
Roof vents	None	None	None	Seven	Nine
Chimney	Short, narrow	Tall, narrow	Tall, wide ¶	Tall, narrow	Tall, narrow
Lights	White over red	White over red	White over red	White over red	White over red ‡
Lamp irons †	None	Two	None when built; two added to some cars later	One ?	Three (fitted by LNER)

† When built, all the LMS Sentinel railcars had a pair of electric lights, one above the other, at each end. Some cars had lamp irons fitted later
* One over engine end and one from seal to trailing end
§ None at engine end; one over door next to seal and one from seal to trailing end
‡ Removed by LNER
¶ No.29910 was fitted with a spark arrester while working on the Wanlockhead branch
    Luggage compartment: In the 'Ripley' car and LMS No.2233, the luggage compartment was at the trailing end. Diagram 1779 also shows the luggage compartment at this end, but the configuration of the production batch of 12 LMS lightweight cars, with additional space either side of the 'seal', as indicated by the panels, is strong evidence of their luggage compartments being at the engine end, as in both the rigid cars.

The only small 'industrial' type Sentinel ever owned by a British main line railway company was LMS No.7164, which was purchased new in 1932 for working at Clee Hill. This picture shows it in its original condition with only a half a back-plate to the cab (not a very cosy proposition for the engine crews at Clee Hill!) with smart painting and lining as delivered by the makers. PHOTOGRAPH: R.M.CASSERLEY COLLECTION

It is possible that an 'industrial' type Sentinel shunters had earlier been tried out at Clee Hill - lightweight shunters had been loaned to the LMS previously (see W/ Nos.5733 and 6735 above), and Clee Hill was not far from the Sentinel factory at Shrewsbury. The locomotive was ordered as LMS Lot 83; it was a small machine, W/No.8593, and was completed in January 1932. It was allotted LMS No.7164, later becoming No.7184. It had a wheelbase of only 4' 9", compared with 7' 0" of the larger LMS Sentinel shunters, was geared for a maximum speed of 9mph, and has usually been quoted as weighing 19 tons, but it is noteworthy that the LMS History Card for No.7164 erroneously lists its dimensions as being the same as the larger engines! No.7164 was delivered in an elaborate non-standard lined-out livery; it worked at Clee Hill until January 1944, and again between January 1946 and February 1947. Although given a Heavy General repair at Crewe in the latter part of 1951, it was then placed in store and withdrawn in December 1955. It was the only example of the small 'industrial' type Sentinel to be owned by any of Britain's main line companies.

The final stage in the LMS involvement with the Sentinel Waggon Works was the ultimate anti-climax. In July 1931, the Shrewsbury firm had engaged Abner Doble, arguably the leading American exponent of the steam car. As a result of this appointment, new designs were prepared for high pressure oil-fired condensing boilers and compound engines. The LMS was at this juncture engaged on trials with various types of diesel shunters, and on 31

March 1933 ordered (as Lot 111) two Sentinel-Doble shunters and, one month later, three Sentinel-Doble railcars. Sentinel allotted these orders W/Nos.8805 and 8806 (the shunters) and 8817-8819 (the railcars), but on 4 April 1934 the orders for one of the shunters and all three railcars were cancelled. This left only one shunter - W/No.8805 - to be constructed; it was an 0-4-0, with a 200hp compound engine, two cylinders (one 4" x 6", the other 7" x 9") driving each axle and a 7' 0" wheelbase. The boiler was an automatic, oil-fired, condensing type, working at 1,500lb/sq.in. pressure. The railcar power units would have been similar, except for a 9' 0" wheelbase. The shunter, LMS No.7192 was taken into stock in December 1934 and, based at Crewe, took part in some comparative trials with the diesels. It was subjected to a series of modifications but, ultimately, its complexity and the inherent design weaknesses ruled it out of consideration, and it was withdrawn in 1943 - no doubt with a sigh of relief from the LMS engineering staff.

The power units for the proposed Sentinel-Doble railcars would have been similar to that fitted to the locomotive, albeit on a 9ft wheelbase. There is one reference in LMS records to the possible employment of the proposed railcars - in March 1934 the District Locomotive Superintendent at Llandudno Junction was in communication with the local branch manager of Shell-Mex & BP concerning the introduction of two oil-fired high pressure Sentinel steam 'coaches' at Bangor. There is no record of any of the earlier Sentinel railcars having worked, or being tried out, in North Wales,

although the L&NWR steam railcars of 1905 and, later, the petrol-electric unit of 1913 had been used in the area. Had the Sentinel-Doble project gone ahead, the use of the railcars in North Wales would have been convenient for supervision from Crewe. But it was not to be and, with hindsight, the LMS's abandonment of the project was a wise move. Several such railcars were actually constructed - these were for overseas customers (and included 600hp compound 2-4-4-2s for the Colombian National Railways) but such was the complexity of their design and their unsuitability for the rough usage inherent in everyday railway operation that they were never wholly satisfactory. No further development was subsequently undertaken.

The LMS Sentinel Railcars - allocation and work

It is unfortunate that very little information has survived concerning the use to which the LMS put its Sentinel railcars, and there is scant photographic evidence to help fill in the blanks. What *does* exist suggests that they may have undertaken brief, and presumably not very satisfactory, trials on a number of lines, in addition to those where there is positive evidence that they ran in revenue-earning service.

When the railcars were introduced in the 1920s it was anticipated that they would offer advantages in economy and reduced running costs, and have the potential to help the railways to beat off the challenge of the motor bus. Railcars were suited to services where the complement of passengers on any one trip would rarely exceed their seating capacity of about fifty - in other words, mainly on rural routes or relatively short urban lines. On the latter, they also provided the facility for quicker turn-rounds, and hence more frequent services than conventional steam trains - other than those worked by motor-fitted locomotives on the 'push-pull' principle. To give further scope for competition, the LMS also fitted their railcars with substantial fixed steps at the passenger doorways so that they could satisfactorily serve wayside stations with lower than normal platforms, but there is no evidence to suggest that any such new 'halts' were actually opened on those lines where the railcars worked.

Experience proved that many of the expectations were illusory, and, worse still, there were unforeseen drawbacks. The lightweight cars were particularly inflexible - lacking drawgear, they could not work in multiple or haul a second coach, or a van; nor could they easily be rescued if they broke down out on the road. They proved difficult to maintain - they represented a new and unfamiliar technology, and in general were deployed in such small numbers that shed staff had little chance to gain the necessary experience to be able to deal with their idiosyncrasies. As with all steam railcars, servicing and maintenance had to be undertaken on shed, alongside locomotives dropping their fires or raising steam, with unavoidable consequences for the cleanliness of their passenger saloons. And, if they *did* succeed, they often created traffic which rapidly exceeded their ability to cope.

The heavier, rigid, gear-driven car should have overcome some of the shortcomings of the earlier lightweight cars. In addition to having better riding qualities, its greater power improved hill-climbing

performance. But the LMS owned only one such car, No.4349 (later No.29913), and can hardly be said to have pursued the possibilities of this 'improved type' with any real enthusiasm. As well as the cars' generally disappointing performance, there was the matter of rough riding, exacerbated by the very small wheels. Not only did the poor quality of the ride deter the travelling public, but it seems to have contributed to the railcars' unreliability and general maintenance problems.

Before examining what little work they did, it is appropriate to consider their competitors. In the late 1920s most of the ex-L&Y and, to a lesser extent, the ex-L&NWR steam railmotors were still in use; more significantly, though, the L&NWR and the Midland had been early exponents - since before the Great War - of push-pull trains and, during the 1920s, such services were being expanded. Indeed, by the end of 1929 no less than 112 ex-L&NWR 2-4-2Ts and 0-6-2Ts were motor-fitted.

Midland Division: As already noted, the LMS's initial trials with lightweight car W/No.5655 were carried out from Derby in 1925, on the service via Little Eaton to Ripley. The first LMS car proper, No.2233 (W/No.6177), probably also had a trial period based at Derby, being used on the Ambergate-Pye Bridge service and in the Chesterfield and Mansfield areas, before being tried out on the Isle of Axholme and then moving to Scotland.

One railcar was reported at Tutbury in September 1932, but this may have been an isolated appearance. At the end of 1934 two of the Sentinel railcars, Nos.29907/11, were in store at Wigston (Leicester), suggesting that they might have worked

on the Midland Division prior to their withdrawal.

One of the LMS's Sentinel railcars was tried out in the 1930s on the Somerset and Dorset, working between Highbridge and Burnham and, possibly, also on the Bridgwater and Wells branches.

Western Division: The only reference to the use of Sentinel railcars on former L&NWR lines is the employment of the proposed Sentinel-Doble cars being serviced at Bangor.

Central Division: After the trials of No.2233 on the Isle of Axholme in 1926, one of the twelve railcars of the 1927 series was, temporarily at least, based at Goole and used on the line before the Axholme's own railcar, No.44, was delivered at the end of 1930.

Elsewhere in the Central Division, in 1933 No.4149 was used the Blackrod-Horwich branch, an old haunt of the L&Y steam railmotors. There had been eighteen L&Y railmotors, but withdrawal had commenced in 1927 and by 1931 seven had already been taken out of service. During the same period, passenger services on several of the routes worked by the railmotors had ceased; it is possible that the Sentinel cars had also been tried on one or more of these branches, although some of the lines in the Pennines incorporated steep gradients with which the Sentinels would not have coped too well.

Northern Division: Many of the main batch of twelve railcars were sent direct to the LMS's Northern Division - i.e. Scotland - in the summer of 1927. This was a shot in the dark. There had been negligible use of steam railmotors in Scotland, and so the LMS had little precedent from which to draw experience. Indeed, in pre-grouping days, only one of the LMS's Scot-

Presumably the engine crews at Clee Hill raised a satisfactory level of protest about the exposed cab on No.7164 when it was new. Additional protection at the rear was eventually provided - this was probably undertaken when the locomotive was in the works in late 1937/early 1938. In August 1939 the locomotive was renumbered 7184. PHOTOGRAPH: F.W.SHUTTLEWORTH COLLECTION

The experimental Sentinel-Doble locomotive, LMS No.7192, had only a short life, being built in 1934 and withdrawn in 1943. It was a most distinctive machine. However, it apparently performed little revenue-earning work during its short life, and we are none too convinced that the duty number (11), seen here, was anything other than an addition for the photographer. PHOTOGRAPH: R.M.CASSERLEY COLLECTION

tish constituents had possessed steam railmotors; this was the Glasgow & South Western, three railmotors having been built in 1904/05 for use on the Cairn Valley line (Dumfries to Moniaive), the branch line from Mauchline to Catrine, and around Ardrossan. They were only moderately successful and were taken out of service by 1917.

The first mention of the activities of the Scottish-based Sentinel railcars was in the October 1927 edition of the *Railway*

Magazine, which reported that, on 22 August of that year, one of the new cars was being used on the Perth-Almondbank-Methven service. The next month's issue listed further Sentinel railcar duties:
Airdrie-Newhouse (2 cars)
Ayr-Dalmellington
Strathaven-Hamilton-Holytown-Coatbridge
There are references to railcars being tried out on the Caledonian branch from Lockerbie to Dumfries in 1928, while in

the summer of that same year No.4149 was in the Highlands, working the Dingwall-Strathpeffer service.

Several were shedded at Dawsholm in 1929, although it is uncertain whether they were used in the Glasgow/Clydebank area, or on the Caledonian/North British Joint line to Balloch, running from the sub-shed at Dumbarton. Two were at Ayr in 1931/32 for the Catrine branch (a one-time G&SWR railmotor route), and at about the same time two others were at Muirkirk.

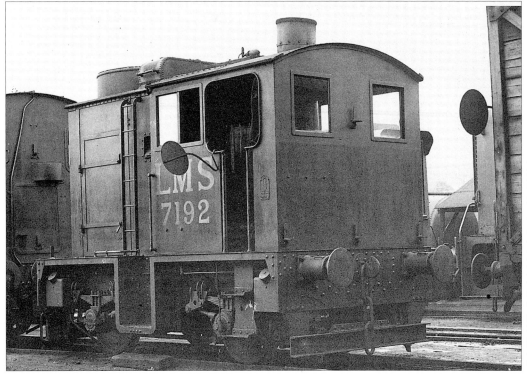

Another view of the unsuccessful Sentinel-Doble locomotive, No.7192. This picture was taken at Crewe South on 19 September 1937 and shows that, since the earlier picture, a taller chimney had been fitted, and there was also an additional housing or cover of sorts on the top of the machine. Here, No.7192 seems to rather neglected, and has been stopped for inspection - at a swift glance, the warning disc looks for all the world like a wing mirror! PHOTOGRAPH: R.M.CASSERLEY COLLECTION

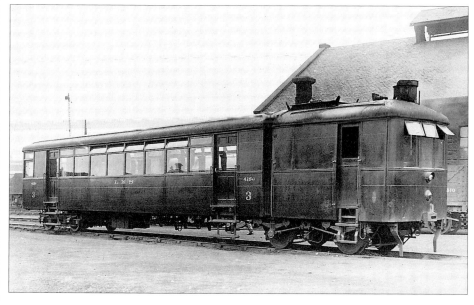

There was clearly a brief period of euphoria. The January 1930 edition of the *Railway Magazine* stated that: '*...the branch services in the Hamilton and Motherwell area are worked to considerable extent by Sentinel-Cammell railcars which are proving useful and popular*'; perhaps, despite their rough-riding and rapid deterioration, they were still an considered to be an improvement on the rolling stock which had hitherto been provided by the Caledonian and the LMS for the inhabitants of the communities in the mining and heavy industrial belt of Lanarkshire!

The September 1930 issue of the *Railway Magazine* reported that the new 100hp Sentinel, No.4349, had been sent to join the other thirteen railcars, all of which were then working in Scotland.

Regarding the use of the Sentinel railcars on the Dalmellington branch, the January 1933 issue of the *Railway Magazine* explained that when they were first employed on the branch in 1927 the service was improved and there were special cheap fares on Saturdays. As a result, passenger traffic regained former levels, but by 1932 the railcars had been largely displaced and were being used only on a single return trip to Ayr.

Despite the early success of the Scottish-based railcars, the LMS withdrew passenger services from a dozen lines in Scotland during 1930 and 1931, along with a number of other closures later in the 1930s. The closures of 1930/31 were:

June 1930: Bonnybridge-Greenhill; Denny-Greenhill; Denny-Larbert (all ex-CR)

December 1930: Airdrie-Newhouse; Holytown-Morningside; Giffen-Kilburnie (all ex-CR); Ayr-Turnberry (ex-G&SWR)

April 1931: Strathord-Bankfoot; Kirtlebridge-Annan (Shawhill) (both ex-CR)

September 1931: Alves-Hopeman; Gollanfield-Fort George; Orbliston-Fochabers (all ex-HR)

The railcars had worked the Newhouse service and they are known to have undergone trials on the Kirtlebridge-Annan line, though on the latter the passenger service was infrequent, and included mixed trains which, of course, the Sentinel railcars could not work. Although the closures didn't di-

Top. Most of the LMS's Sentinel railcars were disposed of in 1935, having had a lifespan of only eight years. One was No.4151, which finished life as No.29909 in the coaching stock lists. This picture, which shows the railcar in reasonable condition, was taken at Perth General probably when it was working the Methven branch. PHOTOGRAPH: ERIC ASHTON COLLECTION

Middle. Several of the LMS Sentinel railcars were based at Ayr. No.4150 was based there during its period of employment on the Muirkirk branch - it is seen on shed at Ayr, presumably *circa* 1931/32. PHOTOGRAPH: R.M.CASSERLEY COLLECTION

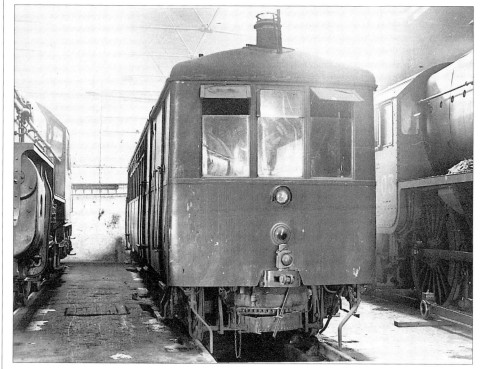

Bottom. A railcar between a Crabs and a Black 5 - No.4143 without lining and in a generally unkempt condition. The location is thought to be Perth shed. PHOTOGRAPH: R.M.CASSERLEY COLLECTION

One of the former S&D Sentinels in newly acquired LMS guise of No.7190 at sunny Radstock on 7 June 1930. PHOTOGRAPH: H.C.CASSERLEY

TABLE TWO: Summary of LMS Sentinel railcars
(a) Articulated 'lightweight' cars; chain drive

LMS Numbers		Built	W/No.	Known allocations and duties	Withdrawn ¶
First	Second				
2233	**29900**	1925	6177	Isle of Axholme 1926; Dawsholm 4.1929; Perth 1932	P 7.1935
4143	**29901**	1927	6781	Perth ?	P 10.1935
4144	**29902**	1927	6780	at Dawsholm 7.1929; Muirkirk 1931-32	P 6.1935
4145	29903	1927	6777	at St Rollox Works yard 7.1929	P 6.1935
4146	**29904**	1927	6782	Ayr 1931-32 (for Catrine branch)	P 6.1935
4147	**29905 ***	1927	6779	Ayr 1931-32 (for Catrine branch)	P 5.1935
4148	**29906 ***	1927	6778	Wanlockhead pre-1933; Hamilton 1933	P 8.1935
4149	**29907**	1927	6786	Dingwall (for Strathpeffer) 5.28; Horwich-Blackrod 1933; stored at Wigston 11-12.1934	P 8.1935
4150	**29908**	1927	6787	Muirkirk 1931-32	P 7.1935
4151	**29909**	1927	6788	at Hamilton 7.1930; Perth pre-1933	P 7.1935
4152	**29910**	1927	6784	Hamilton for Wanlockhead branch 5.1935-6.1936	P 7.1937
4153	**29911**	1927	6785	Dawsholm 4.1929; stored at Wigston 11-12.1934	P 8.1935
4154	**29912**	1927	6783	Goole pre-1931; at Tutbury 9.1932	P 8.1935

(b) Rigid car; geared drive

4349	**29913**	7.1928	7362	Hamilton 1931; Perth (for Methven) 1936; Wanlockhead branch 6.1936-12.1938	P 13.1939

(c) Rigid 64-seat car; geared drive (for Isle of Axholme)

44	**(29987)**	12.1930	8228	Goole (for Axholme) until closure in 6.1933; sold to LNER where it ran as No.51915	7.1944 ‡

¶ LMS withdrawal dates are 'four week period' dates
* Fitted with larger boilers c.5.1929; it is believed that three other railcars (probably including No.29910) also received a larger boiler c.1931
‡ Withdrawn by LNER

Outline history (including 'Ripley' and NCC railcars)

W/No.	LMS Nos. (coaching nos. in brackets)	Built	History
5655	-	8.1924	Trials on Ripley branch 3.1925; returned to Sentinel; trials on LNER 9.1926; sold to Jersey Eastern 1927; to Jersey Railways & Tramways 1929 (regauged to 3' 6"); wdn. 1935
5750	**NCC No.401**	4.1925	Built new for LMS (NCC) 5ft 3in gauge with similar shunter (No.5751); withdrawn 1932
6177	**2233 (29900)**	late 1925	Purchased 7.1926, when order was also placed for 12 new cars; had presumably been on loan for trials since new; withdrawn 7.1935
6777-88	**4143-4154 (29901-12)**	6-7.1927	Nos.29903, 29905 and 29906 given larger boilers 5.1929 (possible three others in 1931); 11 of the 12 withdrawn 5.1935-10.1935; the other, No.29910, withdrawn in 7.1937
7362	**4349 (29913)**	7.1928	On loan for trials from 8.1928; purchased 10.1929; withdrawn 12.1939
7565	-	-	Order cancelled; material used for LNER railcar JOHN BULL (W/No.7822 of 6.1930)
8228	**44 (29987 not carried)**	12.1930	Isle of Axholme Joint Railway high-capacity car; sold to LNER 9.1933; became LNER No.51915; wdn. 7.1944
8817-19	-	-	Sentinel-Doble oil-fired double-engined compound; ordered 3.1933, but cancelled 4.1934 (see shunter W/No.8805)

TABLE THREE: Summary of LMS Sentinel shunting locomotives (mainland)

Numbers and dates applied			Allocation	Built	Works		Final
First	Second	BR	1.1.1948	(delivery dates)	No.	Withdrawn	shed
7160	7180 (8.39)	47180 (by 7.50)	Sutton Oak	1930	8209	7.1953	Shrewsbury
7161	7181 (11.39)	47181 (9.49)	Shrewsbury	7.1930	8210	17.11.1956	Shrewsbury
7162	7182 (6.39)	47182 (12.48)	Ayr	6.1930	8211	2.1956	Ayr
7163	7183 (7.39)	47183 (12.48)	Sutton Oak	7.1930	8212	29.9.1955	Shrewsbury
7164	7184 (8.39)	47184 (11.49)	Sutton Oak	1.1932	8593	10.12.1955	Crewe South
7192	-	-	-	12.1934	8805	1943	-
S&D 101	7190 (6.30)	47190 (4.49)	Bristol	2.1929	7587	7.3.1961	Radstock
S&D 102	7191 (6.30)	47191 (c.52)	Radstock	5.1929	7588	20.8.1959	Radstock

Principal dimensions (list includes locos tried on LMS but not taken into stock)

W/No.	First LMS No.	Type	Cyls.	Boiler pressure	Grate area	H.p.	Wheels	Wheel-base	Weight full
5733	-	Lightweight type; vertical engine	(2) 6¾" x 9"			100hp	2' 6"	7' 0"	15t 0c
5751	NCC 91	Vertical engine; chain drive	(2) 6¾" x 9"	275 lb			2' 6"	8' 6"	20t 0c
6515	-	Vertical engine; chain drive	(2) 6¾" x 9"	300 lb ¶	5.1 sqft	100hp	2' 6"	7' 0"	20t 0c
6735	-	Vertical engine; chain drive	(2) 6¾" x 9"	275 lb	3.97 sqft	200hp	2' 6"	7' 0"	20t 0c *
7587/88	7190/91	Vertical engine; chain drive	(4) 6¾"" x 9"	275 lb		200hp	3' 2"		27t 15c
8209-12	7160-63	Vertical engine; chain drive	(2) 6¾" x 9"	275 lb	5.1 sqft	100hp	2' 6"	7' 0"	20t 17c
8593	7164	'Industrial' type shunter	(2) 6¾" x 9"			100hp	2' 6"	4' 9"	
8805	7192	Sentinel-Doble condensing oil-fired compound	(2) 4" x 6" and (2) 7" x 6"			200hp	2' 6"	7' 0"	26t 4c

* Weight reduced to 14 tons 0cwt for use by LNER
¶ Original boiler pressure 275lb; larger boiler fitted prior to loco's period with LMSR

Outline history (list includes locos tried on LMS but not taken into stock)

W/No.	LMS No.	Built	History
5733	-	6.1925	Trials at Crewe; later returned to makers
5751	NCC 91	5.1925	Purchased with railcar (W/No.5750) for 5ft 3in-gauge NCC lines; withdrawn 1932
6515	-	8.1926	Built for GWR (No.12); returned to maker; trials on LMS 4.1929; returned to maker and resold to T.E.Grey ‡
6735	-	11.1926	Trials at Newton Heath until 2.1928; later went to LNER for trials - taken into LNER stock 1.1929 as No.19; later became LNER No.8139; withdrawn 9.1951
7587/88	7190/91	2-5.1929	Built for S&DJR as Nos.101/102; withdrawn 3.1961 and 8.1959 respectively
8209-12	7160-63	7.1930	Built new for LMS; withdrawn 11.1953 to 11.1956
8593	7164	1.1932	Built new for LMS for service at Clee Hill Quarries; withdrawn 12.1955
8805	7192	12.1934	Remainder of Sentinel-Doble order cancelled; intended to be evaluated with experimental diesel shunters but little used; withdrawn 1943

‡ Now preserved - see text for details

rectly render a number of the railcars immediately redundant, it *did* mean that there was less scope for finding them alternative local employment between their usual turns. Thus, they became inherently uneconomic, even if they performed satisfactorily. Whether or not the Sentinels had been used on any of the other lines which lost their services is uncertain, but they had clearly not been instrumental in promoting the additional passenger traffic needed to keep these routes open. Furthermore, the closures created surplus conventional motive power and rolling stock for use elsewhere and thereby further reduced the scope for the railcars.

Nevertheless, there were two Scottish branch lines which 'enjoyed' the use of Sentinel railcars longer than any of the others. The first was the Methven branch. As already noted, the service from Perth via Almondbank to Methven was one of the first to have been worked by the Sentinel railcars in 1927, and in 1931 a railcar subshedded from Perth inhabited the little shed at the branch terminus. The branch closed to passenger traffic on 27 September 1937, the line having latterly been worked by a Sentinel railcar; it was reported in the contemporary railway press that '...those on board the railcar often wondered whether they would reach the

terminus as the carriage shuddered violently during the final climb, its wheels sinking into every joint'. The identity of this car has not been confirmed, but by this date only the lightweight car, No.29910, and the larger 'improved' car, No.29913 remained in service.

The other branch to retain the services of a Sentinel railcar was the Elvanfoot-Leadhills-Wanlockhead branch in the Lowther Hills in south-west Lanarkshire. This branch had been built under the terms of a Light Railway Order and the stations were devoid of raised platforms - this was also the case at the branch platform at Elvanfoot, the junction with the main line - and, prior to the use of railcars on the branch, the carriages had to be specially fitted with additional steps. Interestingly, in the summer of 1930 an ex-L&Y steam railmotor (LMS No.10608) had been tried on this branch, but without success. The first Sentinel railcar to be used on the branch was No.4148 - one of those with a larger boiler - but it seems that it, too, was not particularly successful, as by 1933 it had been dispatched to Hamilton. Despite previous experience, in May 1935 No.29910 was drafted in, being based at Leadhills shed (the shed, incidentally, was some 1,400ft above sea level - the highest standard gauge engine shed in Britain).

The use of the railcars on the branch reflected the LMS's efforts to keep the line open by cutting operating costs. The branch was geared to the local mining industry, but that had started to decline in the 1920s - inevitably, the rail traffic had declined correspondingly. Competition from road transport was not an issue in this remote part of the Lowther Hills.

While working the Wanlockhead branch, No.29910 was fitted with a spark arrester to reduce the risk of fire on the grouse moors. No.29910 struggled on for a year or more, but was replaced in June 1936 by No.29913 (ex-No.4349), the LMS's rigid, gear-driven railcar. However, the continuing use of a railcar was not enough to save the Wanlockhead branch - the traffic dwindled, and the branch was closed completely at the end of 1938. The final trains had been worked by ex-Caledonian 0-4-4Ts, but the railcar was kept in store for another twelve months, being formally withdrawn in December 1939.

Whilst the Wanlockhead branch railcars worked from the small shed at Leadhills, nominally a sub of Beattock, they were looked after by Hamilton, one of three Scottish sheds which specialised in the maintenance of the Sentinel railcars. Hamilton had also provided the railcars which had been previously used on the other

Nos.47182 and 47183 were the first LMS Sentinels to receive their BR numbers; these were applied in December 1948, along with the BRITISH RAILWAYS lettering in full. (No.47190 was similarly lettered in April 1949). This picture was taken at Ayr on 15 September 1951. PHOTOGRAPH: T.J.EDGINGTON

services in Lanarkshire. It might well have been on the basis of Hamilton's experience with the Sentinel railcars that in the 1940s the shed was lumbered with the LMS's three Leyland railcars, Nos.29950-29952, which seem to have posed even more problems than the Sentinels had done. Given that Beattock shed seems to have little to do with the Sentinel railcars which were used on the Wanlockhead branch, it seems somewhat perverse that the shed looked after the ex-L&NWR steam railmotor which was used on the Moffatt branch; even more perverse, perhaps, is the fact that ex-L&NWR railmotor No.29988, shedded at Beattock, was used on the branch until 1948!

Another 'concentration point' for the Scottish Sentinels was Ayr , which looked after the railcars used on the Ayrshire branches; this was despite the fact that, in the case of the Catrine branch car, Hurlford shed would have been a more convenient base. Ayr, of course, also had its own Sentinel shunter for over twenty-five years. The third Scottish shed to have a continuing association with the Sentinels was Perth, which was responsible for the cars successively used on the Methven branch and possibly elsewhere.

The LMS's Sentinel railcars were, by and large, a failure in Scotland - as, indeed, they were elsewhere. Most lasted for only about eight years, and evidently a number of them spent appreciable periods out of use, in store. It is, nevertheless, apparent that the lightweight, articulated cars were often employed in hilly areas to which they were ill-suited; the low-lying, flat, Isle of Axholme was ideal 'railcar country'. Perversely, the possible advantages of the later type of rigid car were never fully explored, as the LMS had only one example of its own. A not-unconnected issue is why the LMS and the Scottish Re-

gion of British Railways in latter years, did not make greater use of push-pull trains north of the Border? *Prima facie*, there would appear to have been a number of services - for example, the Killin and Aberfeldy branches - for which this method of working would seem to have been very well-suited.

The Sentinel shunters - allocation and work

The LMS's Sentinel shunters were included in Locomotive Stock and, consequently, their movements were more comprehensively documented and are now easier to trace; that said, the surviving Record Cards for Nos.7160 and 7162 (later Nos.47180 and 47182) are not complete and that for the Sentinel-Doble (No.7192) seems not to have survived at all.

As noted earlier, in 1939 five of the Sentinel shunters were renumbered in order to clear a number sequence for new diesel construction. The dates of renumbering are given in Table Three. Under BR auspices they duly had 40,000 added to their numbers - again the dates of renumbering are given in the table.

The four engines delivered new in the Summer of 1930 were allocated as follows:

No.7160 (7180) - no initial allocation is shown (curiously, the same applies in the case of the first LMS 2F 'Dock Tank' No.11270), though one source suggests Inverness. The first entry is its transfer to Northampton in December 1932, where it stayed until at least 1937. It is known that No.7180 (as it then was) had a period at Shrewsbury *circa* 1944/45, but more definite is its transfer to Sutton Oak, the ex-

No.47180 at the top of Clee Hill on 26 November 1951. Next to the locomotive is GW Permanent Way wagon No.30663, inscribed 'Empty to Merthyr'. PHOTOGRAPH: F.W.SHUTTLEWORTH

TABLE FOUR: LMS Sentinel locomotives - allocations and repairs

Notes:
The dates of transfers are LMS/LMR 'period ending' dates

The repair categories quoted are those in use at the relevant time. During the LMS period these were: **S** - shed (running) repair; **LO** - light overhaul; **HO** - heavy overhaul; **LS** - light special; **RS** - running special; **HS** - heavy special; **HG** - heavy general

During the BR period the categories were: **U** - Unclassified; **LC** - light casual; **HC** - heavy casual; **LG** - light general; **HG** - heavy general; **LI** - light intermediate

Prior to mid-1944, the record cards did not show where repairs were carried out.

No.7160/7180:
There is only one surviving record card (an incomplete one) for this locomotive, and so its full history is not known
Allocations: at Northampton 1932-c.1937, but no other details confirmed for period pre-1945; 1.45 - Shrewsbury (probably from 1.44); 2.46 - Sutton Oak; 8.51 - Shrewsbury; **7.53 - withdrawn**
Repairs: 10.36-12.36 (LS); 12.50-3.51 (at Crewe)

No.7161/7181:
Allocations: 12.7.30 - Derby; 26.1.35 - Bromsgrove; 30.11.35 - Derby; 29.2.36 - Gloucester; 16.5.36 - Derby; 3.10.36 - Preston; 18.1.41 - Birkenhead; 10.5.41 - Sutton Oak; 15.2.47 - Shrewsbury; 29.1.49 - Sutton Oak; (loaned to Sheffield, ER, 11.52 to 12.52 and 10.53 to 12.53); 14.5.55 - Crewe South; 6.11.55 - Shrewsbury; **17.11.56 - withdrawn**
Stored: 12.35-1.36; 2.36-5.36; 8.36-9.36; 6.51-11.52; 1.53-10.53; 12.53-1.55; 5.55-8.55
Repairs: 8.35-9.35 (HO); 6.37-7.37 (LO); 7.39-2.40 (HG); 5.42-11.42 (HS); 1.45-1.46 (HG); 3.46-12.46 (LO - Crewe); 1.49-8.49 (HC - Crewe); 12.50-5.51 (HC - Crewe)

No.7162/7182:
Allocations: 16.6.30 - Ayr; **2.56 - withdrawn**
Repairs *(at St.Rollox unless stated otherwise):* 6.36-9.36 (HG); 5.38-6.38 (S - Kilmarnock); 8.38-10.38 (S - Kilmarnock); 4.41-5.41 (LS); 5.41-6.41 (S); 6.41 (S); 7.41 (S); 2.42-5.42 (LO); 2.43-3.43 (LO); 5.44-7.44 (LS); 3.46-7.46 (RS); 9.48-12.48 (LS); 12.50-2.51 (HC - Kilmarnock); 7.51 (U - Kilmarnock); 8.51 (HC - Kilmarnock); 2.53* (LC); 5.53-6.53 (LC); 7.53 (U); 11.54 (U); 12.54 (LC); 1.56 (stored - unserviceable)
* Entry on EHC indistinct - date could be 4.53

No.7163/7183:
Allocations: 12.7.30 - Accrington; 28.9.35 - Lower Darwen; 22.6.40 - Aintree; 22.3.41 - Wigan; 12.4.41 - Preston; 3.5.41 - Patricroft; 17.5.41 - Sutton Oak; 29.1.49 - Shrewsbury; 29.9.51 - Crewe South; 11.7.53 - Shrewsbury; **29.9.55 - withdrawn**
Repairs: 12.30-2.31 (LO); 6.33-8.33 (LS); 6.35 (HG); 9.37-1.38 (LS); 12.39-4.40 (HS); 10.41-3.42 (LS); 11.44-9.45 (HS - Crewe); 2.48-12.48 (HG - Crewe)

No.7164/7184:
Allocations: 13.1.32 - Shrewsbury; 29.1.44 - Sutton Oak; 19.1.46 - Shrewsbury; 15.2.47 - Sutton Oak; 26.3.49 - Preston; 2.4.49 - Sutton Oak; 2.9.50 - Wrexham; 3.2.51 - Sutton Oak; 8.12.51 - Crewe South (in store); **10.12.55 - withdrawn**
Stored: 12.49-5.50; 7.50-8.50; 12.51-withdrawal
Repairs: 11.37-2.38 (LS); 1.44-9.44 (HG); 12.46-10.47 (HS - Crewe); 1.48-3.48 (HO - Crewe); 4.49-11.49 (HC - Crewe); 7.51-11.51 (HG - Crewe)

No.7190:
Allocations: 2.29 - Highbridge (for trials); ? - Radstock; 10.9.38 - Gloucester; 8.10.38 - Radstock; 10.45 - Bristol; 15.3.52 - Radstock; **7.3.61 - withdrawn**
Repairs: 1.30-2.30 (HO); 6.38-7.38 (LS); 9.42-11.42 (HS); 1.46-7.46 (HG); 1.49-4.49 (LI - Derby); 8.51-12.51 (HG - Derby); 8.55-12.55 (HG); 7.58-8.58 (HC)

No.7191:
Allocations: 5.29 - Radstock; 10.33 - Kettering; 12.12.36 - Radstock; c.7.42 - Highbridge; 13.10.45 - Radstock; **20.8.59 - withdrawn**
Repairs: 2.30-3.30 (HO); 11.31-2.32 (HO); 2.33-5.33 (LO); 9.33-10.33 (LS); 11.35-1.36 (HS); 7.36-10.36 (LO); 10.38-1.39 (LO); 9.40-10.40 (LS); 7.43-11.43 (HG); 6.46-9.46 (HS - Derby); 10.51-4.52 (HG)

---

the summer of 1953. No.47182 was, in turn, permanently replaced by ex-LNER Y1 No.68138, the only Sentinel shunter the LNER ever employed in Scotland, which for many years previously had been sub-shedded at Kelso. After its withdrawal in February 1956, No 47182 was cut up at Kilmarnock.

No.7163 (7183) - allocated to Accrington until September 1935 when transferred to Lower Darwen; subsequently allocated to various Central Division sheds (see table), before settling at Sutton Oak in May 1941. During the latter part of the 1940s until mid-1951 three of the LMS's English-based Sentinel shunters were usually based at Sutton Oak simultaneously. In mid-1947, when Nos.7180, 7183 and 7184 were allocated there, the *Railway Observer* reported that their only regular LMS duty was shunting the local Co-op coal yard, although they were often on loan to nearby collieries or other industrial users in the area. A visitor to Sutton Oak on 9 July 1950 reported that Nos.47180, 47181 and 47184 were all on shed and that they '...appeared to be in good condition' - an indication that they were indeed being found useful.

No.7164 (7184) - apart from its routine use at Shrewsbury and, later, at Sutton Oak, the record card notes a couple of weeks at Preston in 1949 and five months at Wrexham in 1950/51. There is also a report of the locomotive being at Monument Lane shed at Birmingham in the early 1950s, presumably for a local trial or maybe on hire to a local industrial concern.

As will be seen from Table Four, apart from the concentration (comparatively speaking!) of Sentinel shunters at Sutton Oak, the other regular long-standing haunt was Shrewsbury, though the locomotives concerned were usually outstationed at Clee Hill for shunting the quarry traffic to and from the top of the incline. The small 'industrial' Sentinel shunter, LMS No.7164, was delivered on 13 January 1932 for duty at Clee Hill, where it replaced one of the veteran ex-L&NWR 0-4-0STs. It continued on these duties until January 1944; thereafter one of the larger LMS Sentinels was more frequently used. The Clee Hill Sentinels were:
1.1932 to 1.1944: No.7164/7184
1.1944 to 2.1946: No.7180
1.1946 to 12.1946: No.7184
2.1947 to 1.1949: No.7181
1.1949 to 9.1951: No.47183
8.1951 to 7.1953: No.47180
7.1953 to 7.1955: No.47183
11.1955 to 11.1956: No.47181
The locomotives sent to Shrewsbury for the Clee Hill job were usually recently ex-works at Crewe. Nos. 47180/83/81, successively, were withdrawn after their last spell at Clee Hill; all three were cut up at Crewe. After the withdrawal of No.47181 in November 1956, its immediate replacement at Clee Hill was one of the former LNER Sentinels, Y3 class No.68164.

Nos.7190, 7191: As already noted, the first of the two S&D Sentinels went new to Highbridge before taking up residence at Radstock, where it was subsequently joined by the second of the pair. The suitability of the S&D Sentinels for working

---

L&NWR shed at St.Helens, Lancashire, in February 1946.

No.7161 (7181) - initially allocated to Derby, moving to Bromsgrove in January 1935; it was, however, photographed inside Burton shed in October 1932 - this was a likely place for it to have been tried out, given that some of the shunting duties in and around the town had severely restricted clearances. At the end of 1935, No.7161 returned to Derby, where it spent some time in store, before transfer to Preston in October 1936.

No.7162 (7182) - initial allocation to Ayr. It remained here until withdrawn in

February 1956. It took over the shunting of the Burns & Laird berth at the harbour, a duty for which a short-wheelbase locomotive was essential. The Ayr Harbour Commissioners had used a Peckett 0-4-0ST (built in 1904) which was taken over by the G&SWR in 1919, becoming their No.735 and later LMS No.16043. In the late 1920s, one of Manson's small 0-4-4Ts was used, until the arrival of the Sentinel. When the Sentinel was away for repair it was temporarily replaced by a small 'Pug' - for example, ex-NBR Y9 0-4-0ST No.68118 deputised in May/June 1951 and ex-Caley 0-4-0ST No.56029 in

The long-standing resident at Ayr, No.47182, on shed in the early 1950s. PHOTOGRAPH: BARRY HOPER COLLECTION

under 'Marble Arch' at Radstock was such that they spent much of their lives in the town - if ever they were unavailable because of repairs, a 'low profile' locomotive (usually a L&Y 'Pug') had to be drafted in as a temporary replacement.

Before long, though, it became clear that there was insufficient work at Radstock to warrant the retention of both Sentinels there, and in October 1933 No.7191 was transferred to Kettering. It nevertheless returned to Radstock late in 1936, but spent much of its time in store. It had a stint at Highbridge during World War II, but returned to Radstock again in 1945 and remained allocated there until being withdrawn (as BR No.47191) in August 1959. Its compatriot, LMS No.7190,

had a brief spell at Gloucester in 1938, and in 1945 it moved to Bristol, principally to work in conjunction with ex-L&Y 'Pug' No.11212 on the Avonside Wharf branch where some of the clearances were rather tight. In 1952 No.47190 (as it then was) returned to Radstock; it saw out its days there, being withdrawn in 1961. The original *raison d'être* for having the Sentinels at Radstock in the first place - namely the low bridge known as 'Marble Arch' - had been demolished the previous year.

Thus, with the exception of the Sentinel-Doble No.7192 which possibly never actually performed any revenue earning duties, the LMS Sentinel shunters all survived until the mid-1950s, each running for well over 20 years. Overall, it would

seem that, apart from the special cases of Ayr, Clee Hill and Radstock, where a Sentinel shunter was employed for twenty-five years or more, the LMS found it difficult to identify suitable permanent jobs for the locomotives. They were tried at perhaps as many as a dozen places, but seldom for long. However, the latter-day concentration of the locomotives at Sutton Oak probably ensured that the best use was eventually made of them.

The LMS Sentinel experience - a verdict

One is left to wonder just how serious the LMS was in its various 'trials' with the products of the Sentinel company and, in this, one cannot help comparing the LMS's experiences with those of the LNER. The LMS took an interest in Sentinel railcars and shunting locomotives at an early stage in their development, and between 1925 and 1929 were never far behind the LNER in their investigations into the potential of these machines. But whereas the LNER established a fleet of eighty-six Sentinel railcars (plus, of course, eleven Clayton railcars) and fifty-eight Sentinel shunting locomotives of three different types, the LMS's fleets were far, far smaller. Furthermore, in the case of the railcars, the LMS had given up on their vehicles in the 1930s, whereas the LNER continued to make perfectly good use of *its* railcars for several years longer.

Then there is the mystery of the first double-engined railcar - did somebody in the LMS hierarchy express an unofficial interest in the concept, but then fail to convince his colleagues sufficiently for this initiative to be followed up? And there is the sad Sentinel-Doble fiasco. This was a radically new development with many untried features - perhaps too many - and clearly had early, enthusiastic support

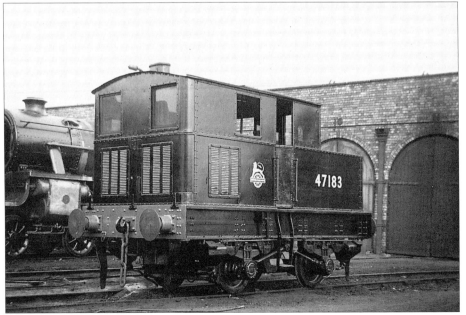

No.47183 with a new coat of paint outside the Crewe Works paint shop on 2 September 1952. This works visit was not noted on No.47183's Engine History Card. PHOTOGRAPH: C.B.GOLDING

At one time or another, most of the LMS Sentinels were allocated to Sutton Oak. The 'industrial' type No.47184 (originally LMS No.7164) had four different stints at Sutton Oak, the last in 1951; it was photographed there on 26 April of that year. PHOTO-GRAPH: H.C.CASSERLEY

from the LMS management, but the cancellation of the whole order except for one shunter doomed the sole representative, No.7192, to failure even before it had been delivered.

The four larger LMS shunters were of a type already reasonably well tried by the time they were received in the summer of 1930. They were to a standard maker's design and lasted in service for much the same length of time as did similar machines purchased by the LNER, albeit with the same kind of maintenance problems, but it should be recalled that these locomotives, like so many of those which

worked on the LMS, were purchased specifically 'for further experiments'.

Between 1925 and 1933, there must have been members of the LMS Locomotive Committee who were sufficiently influential to persuade their colleagues of the potential of the Sentinel range of railcars and shunters. Furthermore, it is worth noting that, despite the controversial Midland bias of the LMS's locomotive department in the 1920s, trials of Sentinel railcars and shunters were undertaken at various locations, notably Crewe (ex-L&NWR section), Derby (former Midland section) and at Newton Heath (on the old L&Y).

However, the whole process was unnecessarily protracted, and decisions took an inordinate time. The LNER had greater success than the LMS with its Sentinel railcars and locomotives, but it must be borne in mind that the former was in a less healthy financial position and, consequently, had a greater need to pursue inexpensive solutions and to persevere with purchases once they had been made.

It is clear that the LMS's experience with the steam railcar of the 1920s and 1930s was generally similar to that of twenty years earlier. Good, reliable, durable designs were rare, and if the railcars succeeded, they often created volumes of traffic which outstripped their capacities and haulage capabilities. The LMS quickly gave them up, and instead continued, except in Scotland, to concentrate on its push-pull services, for which it had plenty of elderly tank engines which could comfortably handle three-coach sets when there was the demand. As for the shunters, the requirement was less than might have appeared as, although the Sentinels could work sidings where there were sharp curves and tight clearances, they were, by and large, unsuited to trip working - for example, taking trains of thirty-odd wagons five or six miles to the nearest marshalling yard.

It was a long and convoluted courtship, but given the obvious tensions within the locomotive management of the LMS before matters were taken in hand with the arrival of William Stanier, the ultimately disappointing outcome of the courtship is not altogether surprising.

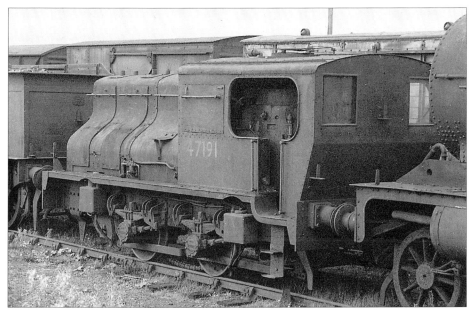

Five of the ex-LMS Sentinels were withdrawn between 1953 and 1956, leaving only the S&D pair, BR Nos.47190 and 47191, in service. The ranks were reduced to just one in August 1959 when No.47191 was withdrawn. The following month - on 24 September - No.47191 was photographed in store at Badnall Wharf, a resting place for a number of withdrawn locomotives, 2½ miles north of Norton Bridge on the Stafford-Crewe line. PHOTOGRAPH: F.W.SHUTTLEWORTH

Author's note: In the preparation of this article, I have been most grateful for the information and advice provided by John Hutchings, whose knowledge of the Sentinel company and its products is unique.

RIVERSIDE REMINISCENCES
by D.Trevor Rowe

Between 1944 and 1948 I worked at the Empire Paper Mills at Greenhithe in Kent. I used to cycle the three miles or so to and from work, and along the route there were various distractions for this young railway enthusiast. My journey took me across the Dartford-Gravesend line which provided sightings of C class 0-6-0s on main-line freights though, after the war, there was sometimes the added attraction of veteran Southern 4-4-0s and ancient 'birdcage' stock on Sunday excursion workings to Allhallows. I then crossed the Gravesend West branch which, being unelectrified, was worked by R and R1 class tank engines and push-

The internal railway system at the APCM works at Swanscombe was converted to the standard gauge in the late 1920s, and five sturdy Hawthorn Leslie 0-4-0STs were ordered for the new set-up. A sixth, similar, locomotive was purchased in 1935. The sixth arrival, W/No.3860, was logically designated No.6 and, in common with the other locomotives in the Swanscombe fleet, it had its number painted on the saddle tanks. This, however, caused considerable confusion in later years as, when the tanks were swapped from one locomotive to another (a consequence of overhauls etc), the numbers were *not* repainted. Thus, what we see here is locomotive No.6 (honest!) - it just happens to have been refitted with the tank from No.3. On 21 August 1967, 'No.6' is seen running through the older part of the quarry and approaching the passing loop near the tunnel. This locomotive is still with us today, having been saved for preservation by the Middleton Railway Trust.
PHOTOGRAPH: PETER GROOM

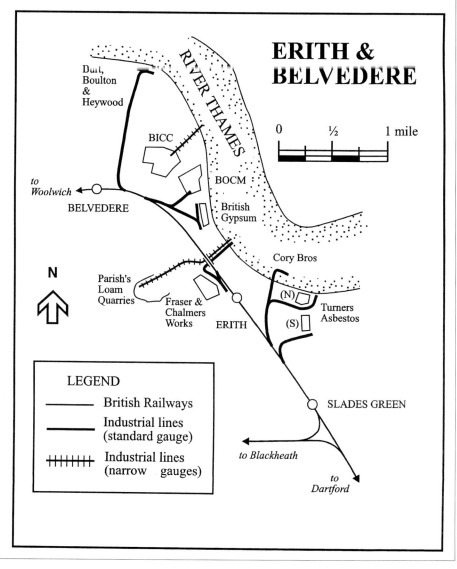

ERITH & BELVEDERE

LEGEND
— British Railways
— Industrial lines (standard gauge)
+++++ Industrial lines (narrow gauges)

In 1948, the Atlas Stone Company near Greenhithe acquired two 0-4-0STs - one from APCM Swanscombe and the other from APCM Kent Works. The latter had been built by Brush Electrical Engineering of Loughborough in 1898 as their W/No.277, and was to remain with the Atlas Stone Co until being scrapped in 1957. It was photographed at the Atlas works in 1949 - the year after its arrival there - and seems to be in rather good cosmetic condition. PHOTOGRAPH: RICHARD CASSERLEY COLLECTION

pull sets. There were also several other railways in the immediate vicinity - these were the industrial lines serving the numerous factories along the Thames estuary, including my own place of work, the Empire Paper Mills.

On my ride to work, the first industrial line I encountered was near the Gravesend West branch. Near the road-bridge, on the right-hand side of the road, was a coal yard, behind which an industrial line struck out

through worked-out chalk pits on a long circuitous journey, serving several industrial concerns (including Bowater's Paper Mills), passing under various roads and the main line to finally reach Bevan's (APCM) works. The fact that this industrial line had connections to chalk pits, paper mills and cement works was somewhat appropriate, as those three industries positively dominated this part of the Thames Estuary.

In keeping with most local industrial concerns, the Bowater's and Bevan's factories at Northfleet both had their own locomotives. At Bowater's, two Andrew Barclay 0-4-0 fireless locomotives were used - one had been built in 1925 and the other in 1928 - but as far as I can remember they did not venture far from the mill. Bevan's Works had more of a railway history - the original railway system was laid to a gauge of 2ft 8½in, though this had

In the 1940s, Bevan's Works at Northfleet had four Peckett 0-4-0STs. One was 'R1' class W/No.829, which had been built in 1900 for Messrs.Hilton, Anderson & Brooks of Halling; it had been transferred to Lee's BPCM Works at Halling in 1931, and moved from there to Bevan's in 1933. At Bevan's Works it was allotted No.4, the number being applied to the chimney, as evidenced in this picture taken on 14 February 1958. PHOTOGRAPH: D.TREVOR ROWE

GREENHITHE & NORTHFLEET

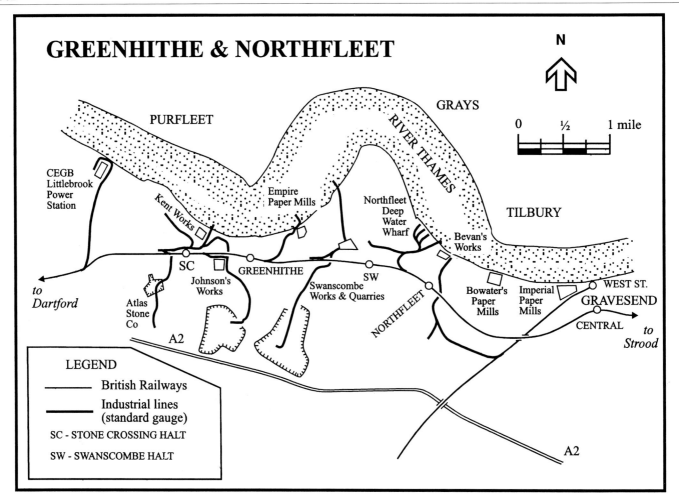

N

PURFLEET

GRAYS

RIVER THAMES

TILBURY

CEGB
Littlebrook
Power
Station

Kent Works

Empire
Paper Mills

Northfleet
Deep
Water
Wharf

Bevan's
Works

0   ½   1 mile

to
Dartford

Atlas
Stone
Co

SC

Johnson's
Works

GREENHITHE

Swanscombe
Works & Quarries

SW

NORTHFLEET

Bowater's
Paper
Mills

Imperial
Paper
Mills

WEST ST.

GRAVESEND

CENTRAL

to
Strood

A2

A2

LEGEND
———— British Railways

━━━━ Industrial lines
(standard gauge)

SC - STONE CROSSING HALT

SW - SWANSCOMBE HALT

been replaced by standard gauge rails in the mid-1920s. When I first became acquainted with the set-up in the mid-1940s there were five locomotives:

• four industrial-type Peckett 0-4-0STs - 'R1' class W/No.829 of 1900, 'M4' class W/No.967 of 1902, and 'W6' class W/Nos.1701 and 1702 of 1926; of these, W/No.1702 (fleet no.2) had been rebuilt with a rear bunker by Bevan's in 1933 but, having found to be poorly balanced, had been rebuilt again in 1946

• Avonside 0-6-0ST- W/No.2001 of 1931 (fleet No.5); purchased from contractors in 1934, but its six-coupled wheelbase proved to be poorly suited to the Bevan's system and so it performed little work before being scrapped in 1951.

Bevan's railway system survived until 1964. Later, when all of the system was moribund, the section between the BR main line near Northfleet station and the riverside formed the basis of a branch which was used by 'merry-go-round' cement trains, but this, too, has since passed into the realms of history and, at the time of writing, there are plans to transform the entire site as part of the Ebbsfleet Channel Tunnel line development.

However, back in the mid-1940s - when these developments were in the future - the tracks of Bevan's system (including some which, even then, had long since been disused) enabled us youngsters to enjoy a circular walk past the flooded quarry, through the tunnels under the main Gravesend-Dartford road, and back via the Bowater's connection to a point not far from where we had started. A few years later, when cycling to work, these tunnels could hardly be seen passing beneath the

main road, although a glimpse was possible from the top deck of a bus.

Continuing along Northfleet High Street I free-wheeled down the steep hill to the Plough Inn, and just beyond here was Northfleet Football Club's ground and the depot of the Northfleet Deep Water Wharf Company. The Deep Water Co had its own internal railway system (it curved under the road and connected with the SR line near Northfleet station), and one of its locomotives had a rather interesting history; this was a Manning Wardle 0-6-0ST (W/No.725 of 1879) which had been purchased by the SE&CR from a firm of contractors in 1904, had passed to the Southern Railway at the grouping to become No.752, and had been sold in 1926 to the Deep Water Co, where it had been named DOLPHIN. Regrettably, I did not actually see this locomotive; by all reports, it had been laid aside in 1943 and, along with another Manning Wardle, was scrapped in 1944 or 1945.

Cycling to work, I pedalled onward over the hill past Swanscombe where the massive APCM Works dominated the scene, the smoke from its high chimneys being perfectly capable of whitening the roofs of houses - and the washing in the gardens! - two or three miles away. The cement works was on the right-hand side of the road and the private railway serving it continued to the river beyond, while to the left of the road, the railway passed under the SR line and on to the chalk pits. There was also a steep, almost spiral, climb to the exchange sidings alongside the SR line. I had the option of an alternative route which avoided the climb to Swanscombe. This was along a dirt track which crossed the

Deep Water Wharf tracks and, later, those of Swanscombe Cement Works, but this was essentially a 'dry weather' route and was not often used. The first internal railway system at Swanscombe Cement Works had been built to a gauge of 3ft 5½in, but had been superseded by a standard gauge system in the late 1920s. By the mid-1940s, when I used to cycle past the works, there were ten locomotives on site, though two or three of these seemed to be almost permanently laid up. The mainstays of the fleet were six Hawthorn Leslie 0-4-0STs, fleet numbers 1 to 6, which had 15in x 22in outside cylinders and 3ft 5in wheels. Four of these survive today in preservation.

And then it was on to my place of employment, the Empire Paper Mills. We had two 0-4-0 fireless locomotives - one a Barclay of 1917 and the other an Orenstein & Koppel of 1907 - which worked around the wharf and mill and also the fairly long branch to Greenhithe station. Beyond here were more cement works with railways of their own, and I sometimes took a stroll along the lineside footpath extending from Greenhithe station to Stone Crossing halt, though, I must confess, at the time I was more interested in main line freights than the industrial scene. Nevertheless, certain industrial activities were noted.

At Greenhithe, to the left, across the SR tracks, was Johnson's (BPCM) Works. Their internal railway passed under the SR main line to reach a river wharf; the line to the river had been electrified in 1928, using the overhead wire system, and was worked by motorised bogie hopper wagons which could carry a 25-ton payload at a constant 7mph. The main system at the works had, like that at some other works

in the area, started life as a narrow gauge set-up (in this case 3ft 9½in), and had been converted to the standard gauge in the late 1920s. By the mid-1940s the steam locomotive fleet comprised ten engines:
• seven Peckett 0-4-0STs, all named - STONE, DARENTH, GREENHITHE, SOUTHFLEET, LONGFIELD (purchased new in 1927/28) and NEW GLOBE and GLOBE No.3 (both transferred from the Globe Whiting Co at Greenhithe circa 1929/30); the first three of the aforementioned locos were delivered with cut-down cabs and lower chimneys
• Bagnall 0-4-0ST named THAMES (transferred from Trenchman & Weekes at Halling in 1935, having been regauged from 4ft 2in prior to transfer)
• Barclay 0-4-0ST named GOLIATH, built in 1921 for Johnson's 3ft 9½in gauge system but regauged in 1927
• Bagnall 0-4-0ST named NEW ELEPHANT, built 1924, also regauged from 3ft 9½in

The 1927/28 Pecketts seemed to do most of the work and, although they were gradually displaced by diesel shunters after the war (and were sometimes sent out on loan to other firms), all five were still at Greenhithe in 1960. DARENTH was scrapped in 1963, but the other four subsequently found further employment elsewhere. One of those was GREENHITHE, which was sold in 1962 to G.&T.Earle for duties at Hessle Quarry in Yorkshire - I saw it there in late 1964, still carrying its old Kentish name.

Over on the river side of the main line was the APCM Kent Works at Stone. Again, motive power was mostly 0-4-0STs - these represented several builders including Brush Engineering of Loughborough (an 0-4-0ST named ELEPHANT) and, allegedly, T.D.Ridley of Middlesbrough (an 0-4-0ST named CLARENCE). However, the truth of the matter is that the latter locomotive seems to have been built, not by Ridley's, but by Andrew Barclay - it is thought that Ridley's had rebuilt the locomotive and, in their customary manner, had put their own works plate on it. Several of the Kent Works 0-4-0STs had been transferred from other works in the APCM combine. There were also three 0-6-0STs, one Hudswell Clarke named STONE (W/No.298 of 1888), and two Manning Wardles, ARTHUR (W/No.1601 of 1903) and APEX (W/No.1657 of 1905); all three 0-6-0STs had been acquired in 1922 from the contractors, Messrs.P.& W.Anderson, who had constructed the cement works.

Another concern at Stone was the Atlas Stone Co, which had taken over part of the system of the Stonecourt Ballast Co. The latter must have been an old established firm as all its

locomotives had been built prior to 1900. Among them was JAMES GOODWIN, an 0-4-0ST which had been built by Alexander Shanks of Arbroath in 1872 and had been acquired secondhand circa 1901. Most of these locomotives were transferred away in 1947 and the remainder scrapped in 1949. There were also two ex-APCM 0-4-0STs - Falcon W/No.205 of 1891 and Brush W/No.277 of 1898 (Falcon Engineering were the forerunners of Brush); both were scrapped circa 1957.

One of the other industrial locomotive operators in the area was the Kent Electric Power Company, which employed two 0-4-0STs - a Peckett of 1939 and a Bagnall of 1946 - at Littlebrook Power Station at Dartford. Interestingly, in 1938 an ex-Lancashire & Yorkshire 'Pug' - latterly LMS No.11257 - had been used by the contractors, Messrs. Holloway Bros, who had been engaged on construction work at Littlebrook Power Station.

Today, all has been swept away, and at the time of writing the site of the Empire Paper Mills was still derelict, although there are now proposals to use the site for a housing development. Until recently there were a few traces of rail in the concrete - this was all that remained of the internal system, once busy with many Grafton steam cranes stacking pulp bales and the two fireless locomotives working up the spur to Greenhithe station or shunting around the mill.

In 1946 I became old enough to work shifts and, although I still cycled to and from work, my journeys were at various times, enabling me to see different activities on the local railways - the SR and the industrial lines - depending on the time of day. My horizons were considerably broadened in 1948 when I left the paper mill and went to work in London, travelling by

train. My daily rail journey took me past numerous rail-connected industrial concerns, most of which have, sadly, long since disappeared without trace.

My journey to London was from Gravesend Central, just a short walk from which was the Imperial Paper Mill, now the site of a supermarket. The paper mill had three 0-4-0 fireless locomotives, the senior pair having been built by Orenstein & Koppel in 1911/12 and the other by Andrew Barclay in 1917; another Barclay fireless was purchased in 1956. The locomotives worked across the road (the extravagantly named Clifton Marine Parade) to reach the riverside wharf adjacent to Gravesend West station and pier; the pier, incidentally, was served by pleasure steamers from London to Southend or Ramsgate.

My train passed the various cement and paper firms near Greenhithe which I had discovered when cycling to my previous place of work. The train journey to London was via Woolwich, and near Erith there was a concentration of industrial railway connections. Right by the station was Fraser & Chalmers Engineering Works, with a pair of smartly turned out Bagnall 0-4-0STs, one built in 1932 and the other in 1945. As we proceeded, more variety was to be found. First came the unusual 4ft 0in gauge line of J.Parish Loam Quarries, which passed beneath the main line; motive power was supplied by two 0-4-0STs, one built by R.& W.Hawthorn in 1891 (W/No.1864) and the other by their successors, Hawthorn Leslie, in 1903 (W/No.2565). Standard gauge industrial railways were represented at Erith by the British Oil & Cake Mills, which had a pair of Aveling & Porter's distinctive 0-4-0 geared locomotives. One of these, SYDENHAM, was a veteran of 1895, while the other, SIR VINCENT, had been built in 1917; both

In 1927, Johnson's Cement Works at Greenhithe purchased three Peckett 0-4-0STs which had cut-down cabs and chimneys to enable them to work through the tunnels. One of the trio was DARENTH (W/No.1741), which was photographed at the works on 2 July 1932. Two further Pecketts were purchased by Johnson's in 1928 - these were built to conventional dimensions, but in later years were rebuilt to a reduced height. PHOTOGRAPH: H.C.CASSERLEY

were eventually saved for preservation. (SIR VINCENT is now in use at the Northamptonshire Ironstone Railway Trust, based at Hunsbury Hill Industrial Museum). Until the arrival of a Ruston & Hornsby diesel in 1953, the Aveling & Porters coped alone with all the BOCM traffic.

Still at Erith, the coal merchants, William Cory & Sons, had a sizeable stud of 0-4-0STs working their standard gauge lines, but it was not a regular contingent as the firm frequently transferred locomotives between its various premises on both sides of the Thames. I often wondered how the locomotives were transferred between the north and south bank of the Thames - in one of the firm's barges, perhaps? In the early 1950s most of the work at Cory's was taken over by diesel shunters; these bore classical names - CIRCE, for example - whereas the steam locomotives bore comparatively plebeian names, often of local towns or those associated with the coal trade. Cory's had been early users of Aveling & Porters, and one of BOCM's pair, SYDENHAM, had, in fact, worked for Cory's until 1924. Cory's wharf was not actually visible from my train, and so was not explored until several years later. The same went for Turners Asbestos Cement Co (a title which would not be at the top of a 'favourite employers' hit parade these days!) who had two works at Erith - the North Works had a Barclay 0-4-0ST and the South Works a small petrol locomotive.

At Belvedere we encountered British Insulated Callenders Cables (BICC), which had an internal 3ft 6in gauge system with a trio of diminutive Bagnall 0-4-0STs. The oldest, proudly named THE MIGHTY ATOM, had been built in 1916 and survived until 1953. The other pair - WOTO, built in 1925, and SIR TOM, built 1925 - survived for longer, and both were ultimately saved for preservation.

After Erith and Belvedere little of industrial interest could be seen from the London bound train, though there were some interesting locations not too far out of sight. In later years, I visited several of

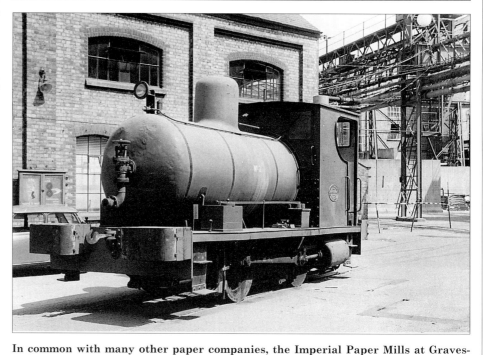

Top. Another Johnson's baby... When the internal railway system at Johnson's Works was converted from a gauge of 3ft 9½in to the standard gauge in the late 1920s, two of the old locomotives were regauged accordingly. One of the pair was Andrew Barclay W/No.1741 GOLIATH, which had been built in 1921. It was photographed at Johnson's on 14 November 1955. PHOTOGRAPH: D.TREVOR ROWE

Middle. Peckett locomotives seem to have been rather popular in North Kent. Another Peckett user in the area was the Northfleet Deep Water Wharf Co, which had a pair of 'R4' class 0-4-0STs; these were W/No.2080 of 1946, named NORTHFLEET, (seen on the right) and W/No.1950 of 1938, named BRADLEY (left). Both survived until the mid-1960s. PHOTOGRAPH: D.TREVOR ROWE

In common with many other paper companies, the Imperial Paper Mills at Gravesend employed fireless locomotives, albeit not exclusively. By the 1940s there were three fireless locomotives on site, and a fourth was acquired in the 1950s. When two of the four were disposed of in the mid-1960s, a singular replacement was subsequently acquired second-hand from the Shell Refining Company. This was Andrew Barclay W/No.1471 of 1916, which had previously worked at Thames Haven refinery. At the Imperial Paper Mills, the locomotive was designated No.2; it was photographed on 14 June 1976, some three years before being cut up for scrap. PHOTOGRAPH: BARRY THIRLWALL

The BOCM works at Erith had two Aveling Porter locomotives, SYDENHAM and SIR VINCENT. They remained on site until the 1960s, and were both subsequently acquired for preservation. SIR VINCENT, seen here at the works on 11 May 1957, had been built in 1917 for Vickers Armstrong at Erith and had been purchased second-hand by the Erith Oil Works (the predecessor of BOCM) in 1931. PHOTOGRAPH: D.TREVOR ROWE

them. There was the Royal Arsenal at Woolwich, which boasted an extensive 1ft 8in gauge system with a substantial fleet of steam locomotives (see *RAILWAY BYLINES magazine 1:4* - Ed). One of the Royal Arsenal locomotives, appropriately named WOOLWICH, can be seen today at Bicton Gardens in Devon. At Charlton, Messrs.G.A.Harvey of Angerstein had an 0-4-0ST new from Robert Stephenson & Hawthorns in 1946, though it was replaced by a diesel in 1954. Also at Charlton was United Glass Bottles, which fielded a 'royal' selection:

• an 0-4-0WT named THE KING; this locomotive was built by E.Borrows & Sons of St.Helens in 1906 and now preserved - to the best of our knowledge, it is destined for the Ribble Steam Railway at Preston Docks

• an 0-4-0ST named PRINCE - this was ex-L&Y 'Pug', latterly LMS No.11243

• an 0-4-0ST named PRINCESS; this locomotive was built by Barclay's in 1898 and was transferred away in 1956.

A little further along the line - though not visible from it - was Greenwich Gas Works, with its fleet of 0-4-0STs (see *RAILWAY BYLINES magazine 3:9* - Ed).

The site of the Greenwich Gas Works is, of course, currently being transformed as a major focal point for the Millennium celebrations, complete with the much talked about Dome, but it is probable that few visitors will associate the site with its former industrial usage. Unfortunately, the same almost certainly goes for the various other industrial sites between Gravesend and London - sites which were once familiar to me as hives of railway activity but, now, have been redeveloped beyond all recognition.

The BICC works at Belvedere had a trio of delightful little W.G.Bagnall 0-4-0STs for duties on the 3ft 6in gauge system. Two of the three - SIR TOM and WOTO - remained in action until 1967, and were later acquired for preservation. This picture shows SIR TOM (W/No.2135 of 1925) in an exceptionally smart condition for an enthusiasts' visit on 20 May 1967. PHOTOGRAPH: PETER GROOM

And finally...

Some of Britain's industrial railways had certain eccentricities. This particular eccentricity could be seen at Fison's peat works at Swinefleet, to the south of Goole - the contraption had been built by placing one locomotive (minus wheels) on the frames of another. As if to add a finishing touch to the 'hybrid', a cab was cobbled together using sheets clipped to plywood sides. But, as they say, beauty is in the eye of the beholder.
PHOTOGRAPH: ADRIAN BOOTH